07454

Da Capo Press Music Reprint Series
GENERAL EDITOR
FREDERICK FREEDMAN
VASSAR COLLEGE

FILM COMPOSERS
IN AMERICA

BOOKS BY CLIFFORD McCARTY

1953 *Film Composers in America: A Checklist of Their Work*

1955 *Music and Recordings, 1955*
    (with Frederic V. Grunfeld, *et al.*)

1965 *Bogey: The Films of Humphrey Bogart*

1969 *The Films of Errol Flynn*
    (with Tony Thomas and Rudy Behlmer)

1971 *Published Screenplays: A Checklist*

1971 *The Films of Frank Sinatra*
    (with Gene Ringgold)

FILM COMPOSERS IN AMERICA

A Checklist of Their Work

By Clifford McCarty

Foreword by Lawrence Morton

DA CAPO PRESS • NEW YORK • 1972

Library of Congress Cataloging in Publication Data

McCarty, Clifford, 1929-
    Film composers in America.

    (Da Capo Press music reprint series)
    "Reprinted with minor additions and corrections."
    1. Moving-picture music—Bibliography. I. Title.
    ML128.M7M3   1972   016.7828   72-4448
    ISBN 0-306-70495-1

First published, 1953; reprinted, with minor additions
and corrections, 1972.

Copyright 1953 by Clifford McCarty

Published by Da Capo Press, Inc.
A Subsidiary of Plenum Publishing Corporation
227 West 17th Street, New York, New York 10011

CONTENTS

x

FOREWORD

The tasks of criticism are many. One of the most altruistic but thankless of them is the gathering together of those materials which make possible the more showy and rewarding tasks.

This book is in the former category. It represents patient labor of the sort that every serious critic of film music has so far shunned, in the hope that somebody else would do it. Meanwhile its need has grown more and more urgent. Now that it has been accomplished one hopes that it will foster further studies concentrating on the plain, bare facts—the statistics—of film music.

There is already, to be sure, a sizable interpretative literature on the subject.* But it is far from comprehensive, it is scattered throughout a great number of periodicals, it is therefore not as accessible as it ought to be and, if the truth be told, it is not very distinguished. Some of it is pertinent but uninteresting, or interesting but fanciful; much of it is mere reportage, spot news; little of it has any permanent value. As opinion, as judgment, it represents a varied assortment of ant's-eye views of film-music events in isolation, a great deal of special pleading, and a still larger amount of prejudiced derogation. Its shortcomings have not prevented it, however, from being made the basis of broad generalizations. These exist, for the most part, as catch-words, epithets, and imprecations. They do not reflect, in any true sense, a general view with either critical or historical perspective. This is not to say that they are false, only that they are partial and hence inadequate.

Something of a general view is given by this book. It will not be seen, perhaps, by those who read the subtitle, *Checklist,* too literally. On the surface it may appear that the editor has done nothing but count the animals as they enter the ark. But let it be acknowledged that no one has had the patience to count them before, and that an enumeration has the value of any set of statistics—it gives the inquiring and analytical mind something to ponder and it raises questions of interpretation.

The inquiring mind might be stimulated by observing some of the phenomena peculiar to the world of film music. The plural authorship of many scores, for instance. Or the assignment of sole credit for a score to a music director who has actually composed none of the music. The film with the anonymous or uncredited score.

---

*See the bibliography, "Literature on Music in Film and Radio," compiled by Robert U. Nelson and Walter H. Rubsamen, in *Hollywood Quarterly,* Supplement to Volume I, 1946; and the Addenda to this bibliography, compiled by Rubsamen, in Volume III, No. 4, Summer 1949. See also Gerald Pratley's "Film Music on Records" in *The Quarterly of Film, Radio, and Television,* Fall 1951 and Fall 1952.

The indestructibility of hacks—their continuous employment and unflagging productiveness. The continent-wide split between the east-coast composers for documentary films and the west-coast composers for theatrical films. The rather infrequent appearance of new composers on the Hollywood scene. The almost exclusive association of certain composers with certain producers or directors, and of certain arrangers and orchestrators with certain composers. The absence of any industry-wide agreement about the meaning and use of such accrediting terms as "Music," "Musical Arrangements," "Musical Adaptations," "Additional Music," "Orchestral Arrangements," "Orchestrations," "Musical Direction," etcetera.

One of these phenomena, the anonymous score, might escape attention because it must be observed, so far as this book is concerned, in absentia. Anyone aware of the high production rate of films in Hollywood may wonder why only some 5200 movies are listed in the Index to Film Titles. What about the missing pictures? They had, most of them, some kind of accompanying music. Presumably that music was composed by someone. But since the identity of the composers has been hidden by the studios, their work cannot be acknowledged here. Four hundred feature films per year is frequently taken as Hollywood's average production. In the 24 years of the sound era (1929-1952, for practical purposes) some 9600 films have been produced—and scored. About 4400 scores might thus be classified as anonymous. They will doubtless remain so until studio music libraries are opened to the research worker.

Many of these scores, especially those of the early 'thirties, were created not by individual composers but by a music staff working under the supervision of a music director. They collaborated in a practical way by using common thematic material and employing one or another of the currently fashionable styles—the neo-Gershwin, for instance, the western folk, or the Wagner-Strauss symphonic. In many of these scores, collaboration was a very successful procedure from the standpoint of music-department operation and theatrical effectiveness, whatever the strictly musical results may have been. Screen credit, if it was given at all, usually went to the music director, though there were exceptions, as in Stagecoach and Union Pacific, where plural authorship was acknowledged on the screen.

As late as 1936 George Antheil described the production of these anonymous-composite scores as though it were the normal procedure in the studios.* It is not normal today, though it may be revived from time to time in order to meet emergencies such as tax dates, release dates, and commitments of composers or orchestras to other films. But where the practice still persists in a somewhat modernized version is in the scoring of low-budget films produced by the major studios. Here there are vast libraries of music previously composed for feature pictures. From such a library a music director extracts

*George Antheil, "Breaking Into the Movies," in Modern Music, January 1937, p. 82-86.

the choicest bits and combines them into a melange according to the requirements of the film he is scoring. He himself may even compose a few bars of music for connective tissue here and there, and he may conduct the studio orchestra in the recording of this pastiche. Some of these paste-pot-and-scissors scores are indeed skillfully made; oftentimes they are tailored to the film as nicely as a specially composed score, though the variety of musical styles in any one of them might offend the sensitive listener. There is little evidence, however, that audiences are any more aware of these faults than they are of the virtues of the most distinguished scores. The goal of the paste-pot-and-scissors score is not musical integrity but dramatic aptness at the smallest possible cost. One does not lament the anonymity of these compiled scores; but their absence from this book should be explained. It should be noted, incidentally, that the music directors of these scores usually receive screen credit.

I digress here momentarily to remind readers that the paste-pot-and-scissors tradition is not as shocking as purists like to pretend. Its most immediate precedent, which many people nowadays contemplate with nostalgic pleasure, is the kind of film scoring practiced in the days of silent films, when bleeding chunks of Grieg, Tchaikovsky, Beethoven, and Schubert, and of Borch, Becce, Rapee, and Zamecnik were strung together by organists and pit-orchestra leaders with a magnificent indifference toward the incompatibility of opposing musical styles. But there is also an older precedent in pasticcio opera of the eighteenth century. The parallel between opera of this period and modern film scoring has been drawn more than once. Pasticcio opera has become a very respectable subject for musicological discourse, and Frank Walker's brief study of *Orazio** is only the most recent proof that many a knee-breeched impresario would have to change only his costume to feel perfectly at home in the music department of a modern Hollywood studio. *Orazio* held the boards for two decades in a dozen European cities, its music being ascribed with more or less inaccuracy to Latilla, Pergolesi, Auletta, and Galuppi, as well as to *Diversi* or to nobody at all. This sounds very interesting nowadays, since history has a way of transfiguring yesteryear's trivia into *memorabilia*. It is therefore not altogether ridiculous to imagine that two or three centuries hence some eager young candidate for a Ph. D. in musicology might earn his degree by searching through the atomic rubble of Hollywood for evidence of the many purposes served by Alfred Newman's music for *Street Scene* or Hugo Friedhofer's for *The Bandit of Sherwood Forest* during The Golden Age of Film Music.

As the reader will have observed, most of the statistician's problems are posed by the accreditation policies of the studios. They have a rather whimsical history. Almost from the beginning of the sound era it was studio practice to give screen credit to music direc-

---

*Frank Walker, *"Orazio*: The History of a Pasticchio," in *The Musical Quarterly*, July 1952, p. 369-383.

tors. It appears that the late Leo Forbstein, head of the music department at Warner Brothers, received such credit on nearly every Warner feature film from 1929 until his death in 1948. After 1935 composer's credit was given to top-bracket composers. M-G-M gave some music-director and composer credits from 1929, have given all since 1934. At 20th Century-Fox, music directors were credited from 1933, composers consistently from 1942. Paramount gave few music credits of any kind until 1936, when music directors were credited; composer credits became usual in 1939. At RKO, music directors and composers received credit from 1931. At Columbia, Morris Stoloff has received music-director credit since 1936; composer credits have been common since 1939. Although Universal has given some credits since 1934, only from 1946 have composers been consistently credited. Republic began crediting musical directors in 1936, composers consistently in 1948. All of these dates are approximate, and there have been exceptions to the general rule at nearly all of the studios. It might be said with reasonable inaccuracy that only since about 1939 has there been any industry-wide inclination toward consistency in the accreditation of composers. That inclination has not yet become confirmed practice. Arrangers and orchestrators continue to work in comparative obscurity.

This whole question is badly in need of the kind of solution worked out by the Screenwriters' Guild for its members. A system of accreditation for writers is embodied in the basic labor agreement between the Guild and the studios. It includes a method for the arbitration of disputes over credits. As a result of this machinery, screen credits for writing are generally accurate and they mean what they say. Composers, however, are not organized in any labor union, and credit for work done is a matter of individual negotiation between the composer and his employer. Arrangers and orchestrators, on the other hand, are under the jurisdiction of the American Federation of Musicians. But the Federation has never made any distinction between arranging and orchestrating, which are two very different jobs. Actually the union considers them identical even in its basic wage agreement with the studios; and it has never set up any kind of accrediting system at all.

While the inaccuracy of credits creates real problems for the researcher, as the editor of this volume points out with admirable detachment in his Preface, these are not the problems to which I would call attention here. Ostensibly, credit lists tell audiences who is responsible for the jobs generally regarded as "creative." But their real importance lies not in what they tell the public but in what they tell the industry. Credits are a gauge of an artist's standing in his profession, and they weigh heavily when he is a candidate for a job. "What are your credits?" is likely to be the first question a producer or director asks the job-seeking composer. To the greater number of employers, a significant credit is a credit for work done on a successful picture. The composer of a score consisting of six minutes of trash for a box-office hit has a more significant credit than the composer of 40 minutes of first-class music for a box-office failure. Naturally, the composer with the most significant *credits* is hired in preference to the composer with the most significant *talent,* since most of those who do the hiring are more skilled in judging box-office reports than in judging music. This book makes it devastatingly plain that far more scores have been composed by hacks and quacks than by genuinely creative composers, though plenty of the latter are available. All composers, good and bad alike, must be jealous of their screen credits. They must be looked upon as economic assets, as a record of the quantity of their work (that is, of the amount of their experience); as a record of their association with particular studios, producers, directors, or stars; as a record, in short, of how they rate in Hollywood. In a sense, this book is a social register of film composers.

For those who are genuinely interested in film music, either as participants or as critical observers, this book performs another service: it charts the whole territory for the first time. Every reader will, according to his lights and the extent of his experience with film music, make his own checklist of worthwhile scores. For some, the area worth examining further will be vastly increased; for others it will be drastically reduced. All will probably attempt some sort of evaluation of the whole field, on the basis of such criteria as the reputations of the composers, their successes in other fields of music, scores and pictures remembered, personal taste, opinions current in the critical market place, *etcetera.* But whatever criteria are applied, it is likely that there will be general agreement on one point: that the vast majority of film scores are negligible. This should not be surprising in a world where the vast majority of symphonies and sonatas, novels and short stories, poems, paintings and sculpture are also negligible. In the world of the plastic gadget, honest wood and metal are likely to be self-conscious and embarrassed. If this is not surprising, it is still regrettable. Especially in film music, since good scores can be had at no greater cost than bad ones.

This failure of the film industry cannot be excused. But it can be explained. Film music does not have to be good in order to perform its functional duties. Except in rare instances, it has nothing to do with art. It could, and one hopes for the day when it will. In the meantime it has everything to do with commerce. Above all, it must be successful — that is, it must "do something for the picture," please whoever is paying for it and, if possible, win an "Oscar." The film producer does not exist who would not sacrifice even the greatest music if he believed that such a sacrifice would ensure the success of his film. Indeed, some of the greatest music, from Bach's to Debussy's, has already been so sacrificed. This is something of an anomaly in an industry where first-rate achievement is permitted, even encouraged, in certain other departments — photography, for instance, or costume and set designing.

In the midst of so much musical mediocrity, optimists have all the more reason for being grateful that good scores prove to be as numerous as they are. But it must be kept in mind that the goodness of a score will not be detected by those who evaluate film music according to wrong criteria. Concert-hall and opera-house standards are as irrelevant to film music as they are to one another. Film music has its own standards. These are not theoretical; they have been established by example and tested in the theater. Certainly it has been proved that although film music does not have to be good in order to fulfil its function, good music actually performs that function far more satisfactorily than bad music. The worst that can be said about most film music is that it does not live up to its own best standards.

This truth must be constantly hammered at producers who hire hacks when artists are available. Criticism has been laggard in the performance of this job. Producers will rest content so long as movie critics, like the movie-going public itself, continue to exhibit their altogether remarkable insensitivity to all film music except popular songs, folk tunes, ballads, or familiar concert and opera classics; and so long as music critics continue to ignore film music completely. The need for intelligent and rigorous film-music criticism remains as urgent, and as unsatisfied, as it has been for twenty years. This book, testifying to the supremacy of mediocrity, is a clarion call to criticism. At the same time it testifies to the stubbornness and persistence of virtue. Good film scores may indeed be an overwhelmed minority, but they shine like good deeds in a naughty world.

LAWRENCE MORTON

Beverly Hills, Calif.
March, 1953

EDITOR'S PREFACE

This is neither a history nor a critique of film music. It is a reference book and represents an attempt to do for film composers what bibliographies do for authors — provide a record of their work, both important and insignificant. Following the names of the 163 composers who appear here alphabetically are lists of the American motion pictures — features, shorts, documentaries and experimental films — for which they composed the musical scores.

Although these lists are based primarily on screen credits, it should be noted that screen credits are not always accurate, usually not for what they include but for what they omit. How much information appears on the screen is a matter of studio policy, and until comparatively recently most studios were reluctant to give credit other than to a music director. So when composers are credited here with pictures for which they received no screen acknowledgment, such credits were established by correspondence with the composers themselves.

Naturally, many books and periodicals were consulted also, the most important of which are: *Motion Picture Production Encyclopedia, The Film Daily Year Book, International Motion Picture Almanac, Motion Pictures: 1912-1939 (Catalog of Copyright Entries), Music and Dance in California, Variety, Motion Picture Herald, The Hollywood Reporter, The Film Daily, Films, The Quarterly of Film, Radio, and Television* (formerly *Hollywood Quarterly*). *Overture, The Score* and *Film Music* (formerly *Film Music Notes*). Information in these publications often is inaccurate, however, and each title in this book had to be checked and re-checked against all available references to establish its authenticity.

Sometimes during the production of a picture, after the credited composer has completed his assignment, either the general music director or the producer may decide that additional music is needed, either to supplement or to replace the original score. The added music may total only a few bars or sequences, and the composer rarely gets screen credit. However, it is common knowledge in the industry that on more than one occasion a major portion of a score has been replaced by music of composers other than the one credited. After the release of *The Heiress* in New York, Aaron Copland found it necessary to address a letter to the press denying responsibility for the main title music which was substituted for his own work. A situation of this sort is only one of the problems confronting the reasearcher, and he is inclined to wonder how many such cases will forever remain undetected.

On musicals a composer usually receives credit for "musical direction," a term described by Adolph Deutsch as including "all such musical functions as adapting, arranging, conducting, composing background music, and general responsibility for the entire musical content of the picture with the exception of composing the songs." However, the term "musical direction" does not mean the same at all studios. Its appearance on the screen as the sole music credit does not imply that the musical director also composed the score, though this often is the case, just as credit for the score does not necessarily mean that the composer conducted his own music, though this is not uncommon.

Credits for orchestrations, arrangements, adaptations, and additional composition, though not intended as an integral part of this book, nevertheless have been included, when available, following the titles of the pictures to which they belong. An Index of Orchestrators will be found on page 191. Nearly all film composers employ orchestrators, the most notable exception being Bernard Herrmann.

In the Index of Film Titles, a title is followed by the page on which will be found all available credits for that picture. In the text, a title is listed under the composer with the most important credit, *i.e.,* composition or musical direction. However, if the *only* available credit for a film is one for orchestration or arrangements, the title appears under the composer receiving such credit. Each composer's list of scores appears in chronological order of release, not of composition.

As to omissions and mistakes herein, the only apology offered is this sympathetic statement by the noted musicologist, Otto Erich Deutsch: "One wonders ruefully, in view of the inevitable errors which occur in first editions of such catalogues, whether works of this kind ought to appear in second editions only!"

The scope of this book does not permit inclusion of the work of conductors, song writers and vocal arrangers. Neither has an attempt been made to indicate the lengths of scores. A composer may have written music only for the main and end titles, or he may have underscored the entire picture. It should be remembered that a composer's score passes through the hands of orchestrators, sound engineers, dubbers, the general musical director and the producer, each of whom can exert a determining effect on the sound of the music you hear in the theater.

ACKNOWLEDGMENTS

Most of the research for this book was done at the Library of the Academy of Motion Picture Arts and Sciences, and grateful acknowledgment is due Miss Elizabeth C. Franklin and Miss Lillian N. Schwartz of that admirable institution for their generous assistance.

My thanks go also to MCA Artists, Ltd., Agency, the Publicity Department of Warner Brothers Studio, Mr. George G. Schneider of Metro-Goldwyn-Mayer, and to the many composers who answered inquiries concerning their work and who revised and approved their lists for publication.

ABBREVIATIONS

PRODUCING AND DISTRIBUTING ORGANIZATIONS

AA .... Allied Artists
A.A.F. .... Army Air Forces
Col .... Columbia
EL .... Eagle Lion
FC .... Film Classics
GN .... Grand National
MGM .... Metro-Goldwyn-Mayer
O.W.I. .... Office of War Information
Par .... Paramount
PRC .... Producers Releasing Corp.
Rep .... Republic
RKO .... R K O Radio
SG .... Screen Guild
20th .... 20th Century-Fox
T-S .... Tiffany-Stahl
UA .... United Artists
UI .... Universal-International
UPA .... United Productions of America
Univ .... Universal
WB .... Warner Bros.-First National

MUSICAL FUNCTIONS

A .... Arrangements
AC .... Additional Composition
C .... Compilation
MA .... Musical Adaptation
MD .... Musical Direction
O .... Orchestration
PS .... Part Score

JOSEPH ACHRON

1935 *Spring Night* (short; O: Powell)   Paramount

DANIELE AMFITHEATROF

1939	*The Ash Can Fleet* (short)	MGM
	A Failure at Fifty (short)	MGM
	Fast and Furious	MGM
1940	*The Man from Dakota* (with Snell)	MGM
	And One Was Beautiful	MGM
	Keeping Company	MGM
1941	*The Get-Away*	MGM
1942	*Joe Smith, American*	MGM
	Calling Dr. Gillespie	MGM
1943	*Dr. Gillespie's New Assistant*	MGM
	Andy Hardy's Double Life	MGM
	Northwest Rangers (with Snell)	MGM
	A Stranger in Town (with Shilkret)	MGM
	Aerial Gunner	Pine-Thomas-Par
	High Explosive	Pine-Thomas-Par
	Harrigan's Kid	MGM
	Dr. Gillespie's Criminal Case	MGM
	Lassie Come Home	MGM
1944	*Lost Angel*	MGM
	Cry Havoc	MGM
	Days of Glory (O: Raab)	RKO
1945	*I'll Be Seeing You*	Selznick-RKO
	Guest Wife	Skirball-UA
1946	*Miss Susie Slagle's*	Paramount
	The Virginian (O: Cutner, Shuken)	Paramount
	Suspense	King Bros.-Mon
	O.S.S. (with Roemheld; O: Cutner, Shuken)	Paramount
	Song of the South	Disney-RKO
	(Photoplay only; cartoon score: Smith; O: Plumb)	
	Temptation	UI
1947	*The Beginning or the End* (O: Cutner, Shuken)	MGM
	Smash-Up—the Story of a Woman (O: Tamkin)	UI
	Ivy (O: Cutner, Shuken, Tamkin)	UI
	Singapore (O: Tamkin)	UI
	The Lost Moment (O: Tamkin)	UI
1948	*The Senator Was Indiscreet* (O: Tamkin)	UI
	Letter from an Unknown Woman (O: Tamkin)	UI
	Another Part of the Forest (O: Tamkin)	UI
	Rogues' Regiment (O: Tamkin)	UI
1949	*You Gotta Stay Happy* (O: Tamkin)	UI
	An Act of Murder (O: Tamkin)	UI

	The Fan (O: De Packh, Powell)	20th
	Sand (O: De Packh, Powell)	20th
	House of Strangers (O: De Packh)	20th
1950	*Backfire* (O: Cutner, Shuken)	WB
	Under My Skin (O: De Packh, Hagen)	20th
	The Capture (O: Tamkin)	Showtime-RKO
	The Damned Don't Cry (O: Cutner, de Packh, Shuken)	WB
	Devil's Doorway (O: Tamkin)	MGM
	Copper Canyon (O: Cutner, Shuken)	Paramount
1951	*Storm Warning* (O: De Packh)	WB
	Bird of Paradise (O: Powell)	20th
	The Painted Hills	MGM
	Goodbye, My Fancy	WB
	Angels in the Outfield	MGM
	Tomorrow Is Another Day (O: De Packh)	WB
	The Desert Fox (O: De Packh)	20th

GEORGE ANTHEIL

1935	*Once in a Blue Moon*	Paramount
	The Scoundrel	Paramount
1936	*The Plainsman*	Paramount
1937	*Make Way for Tomorrow* (A: Young)	Paramount
1938	*The Buccaneer* (AC: Carbonara, Roder)	Paramount
1940	*Angels Over Broadway*	Columbia
1946	*Specter of the Rose* (O: Maxwell)	Republic
	Plainsman and the Lady (O: Butts, Gold, Scott)	Republic
	That Brennan Girl (O: Gold)	Republic
1947	*Repeat Performance*	Eagle Lion
1949	*Knock on Any Door* (O: Gold)	Santana-Col
	We Were Strangers (O: Gold)	Horizon-Col
	The Fighting Kentuckian (O: Butts)	Republic
	Tokyo Joe (O: Gold)	Santana-Col
1950	*House by the River* (O: Butts)	Fidelity-Rep
	In a Lonely Place (O: Gold)	Santana-Col
1951	*Sirocco*	Santana-Col
1952	*The Sniper*	Kramer-Col
	Actors and Sin (O: Gold)	Kuller-UA
1953	*The Juggler* (O: A. Morton)	Kramer-Col

LOUIS APPLEBAUM

1944	*Tomorrow, the World*	Cowan-UA
1945	*Story of G. I. Joe*	Cowan-UA

2

1948   *Dreams That Money Can Buy*   Films Intl. of America
       (with Bowles, Cage, Diamond, Milhaud)
1949   *Lost Boundaries*   De Rochemont-FC
1950   *Farewell to Yesterday* (documentary)   20th
       (with Robert McBride, Richard Mohaupt)
1951   *Teresa*   **MGM**
       The Whistle at Eaton Falls   De Rochemont-Col
Also many documentaries and other films outside U. S., including 42 for the National Film Board of Canada.

LEO ARNAUD

1946   *The Thrill of Brazil*   Columbia

WILLIAM AXT

1925	*The Big Parade* (with Mendoza; O: Baron)	MGM
1926	*Ben-Hur* (with Mendoza; O: Baron)	MGM
	Don Juan (with Mendoza; O: Baron)	**WB**
1928	*White Shadows in the South Seas* (with Mendoza)	MGM
	Our Dancing Daughters (with Mendoza)	MGM
1929	*The Trail of '98* (with Mendoza)	MGM
	Thunder	MGM
	The Single Standard	MGM
	Our Modern Maidens	MGM
	Speedway	MGM
	The Kiss	MGM
1932	*Polly of the Circus*	MGM
	The Wet Parade	MGM
	Sea Spiders (short)	MGM
	Washington Masquerade	MGM
	Smilin' Through	MGM
1933	*The Secret of Madame Blanche*	MGM
	Gabriel Over the White House	MGM
	Reunion in Vienna	MGM
	Midnight Mary (A: Maxwell)	MGM
	Storm at Daybreak	MGM
	Penthouse	MGM
	Broadway to Hollywood	MGM
1934	*Dinner at Eight*	MGM
	Eskimo (O: Marquardt)	MGM
	You Can't Buy Everything	MGM
	This Side of Heaven	MGM
	Lazy River	MGM

	Men in White	MGM
	Manhattan Melodrama	MGM
	Sadie McKee	MGM
	The Thin Man	MGM
	Operator 13	MGM
	The Girl from Missouri	MGM
	Straight Is the Way	MGM
	Hide-Out	MGM
	A Wicked Woman	MGM
	Forsaking All Others	MGM
1935	*The Murder Man*	MGM
	Woman Wanted	MGM
	Pursuit	MGM
	O'Shaughnessy's Boy	MGM
	It's in the Air	MGM
	Rendezvous	MGM
	The Perfect Gentleman	MGM
	Whipsaw	MGM
1936	*Three Live Ghosts*	MGM
	Tough Guy	MGM
	The Perfect Set-Up (short)	MGM
	The Garden Murder Case	MGM
	The Three Godfathers	MGM
	Petticoat Fever	MGM
	The Unguarded Hour	MGM
	The Three Wise Guys	MGM
	We Went to College	MGM
	Suzy	MGM
	Piccadilly Jim	MGM
	Old Hutch	MGM
	Libeled Lady	MGM
	All American Chump	MGM
	Mad Holiday	MGM
1937	*Under Cover of Night*	MGM
	The Last of Mrs. Cheney	MGM
	Espionage	MGM
	Song of the City	MGM
	Parnell (O: Bassman, Marquardt)	MGM
	Between Two Women	MGM
	London by Night	MGM
	Big City	MGM
	Thoroughbreds Don't Cry	MGM
	Beg, Borrow or Steal	MGM
	The Bad Man of Brimstone	MGM
1938	*Friend Indeed* (short)	MGM

4

	MGM
Everybody Sing	MGM
(MD; A: Edens; O: Arnaud, Bassman, Cutter)	MGM
The First Hundred Years	MGM
Yellow Jack	MGM
Woman Against Woman	MGM
Fast Company	MGM
Rich Man, Poor Girl	MGM
Three Loves Has Nancy	MGM
Listen, Darling (A: Edens)	MGM
Spring Madness	MGM
The Girl Downstairs	MGM
1939 *Stand Up and Fight*	MGM
Pygmalion (AC; score: Honegger)	MGM
Within the Law	MGM
Sergeant Madden	MGM
The Kid from Texas	MGM
Tell No Tales	MGM

GEORGE BASSMAN

1940	*Too Many Girls* (O: Bassman, Rose)	RKO
1943	*Young Ideas*	MGM
	Whistling in Brooklyn	MGM
1944	*The Canterville Ghost*	MGM
1945	*Main Street After Dark*	MGM
	The Clock (O: Cutner, Duncan, Shuken)	MGM
	Abbott and Costello in Hollywood (O: Duncan)	MGM
1946	*A Letter for Evie* (O: Sendrey)	MGM
	The Postman Always Rings Twice	MGM
	(O: Duncan, Franklyn, Sendrey)	
	Two Smart People (O: Sendrey)	MGM
1947	*Little Mister Jim* (O: Duncan, Franklyn, Sendrey)	MGM
	The Romance of Rosy Ridge	MGM
	The Arnelo Affair (O: Cutner, Shuken)	MGM
1950	*Japan and the World Today* (documentary)	U. S. Govt.

ROBERT RUSSELL BENNETT

SCORE:

1938	*Fugitives for a Night*	RKO
	Annabel Takes a Tour	RKO
1939	*Pacific Liner*	RKO
	Career	RKO
	Fifth Avenue Girl	RKO

ORCHESTRATION:

1936	*Show Boat*	Universal
1937	*High, Wide and Handsome*	Paramount
	Hitting a New High (with Bassman)	RKO
1938	*Joy of Living*	RKO
1939	*The Story of Vernon and Irene Castle*	RKO
1947·	*Carnegie Hall*	Federal-UA

ELMER BERNSTEIN

1951	*Saturday's Hero*	Buchman-Col
1952	*Boots Malone*	Buchman-Col
	Sudden Fear	Kaufman-RKO
1953	*Battles of Chief Pontiac*	Broder-Realart
	Never Wave at a Wac	Independent Artists-RKO

MARC BLITZSTEIN

1931	*Surf and Seaweed*	Ralph Steiner
1936	*Chesapeake Bay Retriever*	Pedigreed Pictures
1937	*The Spanish Earth*	Contemporary Historians
	(music arranged with Virgil Thomson)	
1940	*Valley Town*	Willard Van Dyke
1941	*Native Land*	Frontier Films
1942	*Night Shift*	O.W.I.

PAUL BOWLES

1933	*Siva*	Central Films
1934	*Innocent Island*	Harry Dunham
1935	*Venus and Adonis*	Harry Dunham
1936	*145 West 21*	Rudolph Burckhardt
	Seeing the World; A Visit to New York	Burckhardt
1937	*America's Disinherited*	Sharecropper Committee
1938	*Too Much Johnson*	Orson Welles
	How to Become a Citizen of the United States	Burckhardt
	Chelsea Through the Magnifying Glass	Burckhardt
	The Sex Life of the Common Film	Burckhardt
1939	*Film Made to Music Written by Paul Bowles*	Burckhardt
1940	*Roots in the Earth*	Dept. of Agriculture
1944	*The Congo*	Belgian Govt.
1948	*Dreams That Money Can Buy*	Films Intl. of America
	(with Applebaum, Cage, Diamond, Milhaud)	

SCOTT BRADLEY

1946	*Courage of Lassie* (with Kaper) (AC, O: Cutner, Sendrey)	MGM
1950	*The Yellow Cab Man* (O: Franklyn, Sendrey)	MGM

Also hundreds of MGM and Harman-Ising cartoons.

JOSEPH CARL BREIL

1911	*Queen Elizabeth*	Paramount
1915	*The Birth of a Nation**	Griffith
1916	*Intolerance*	Griffith
1923	*The White Rose*	Griffith

DAVID BROEKMAN

1925	*The Phantom of the Opera*	Universal
1929	*Mississippi Gambler*	Universal
	Tonight at Twelve	Universal
1930	*Outside the Law*	Universal
	All Quiet on the Western Front	Universal
1931	*Frankenstein*	Universal
1934	*Gimme My Quarterback*	Educational

DAVID BUTTOLPH

MUSICAL DIRECTION:

1935	*This Is the Life*	20th Century-Fox
	Navy Wife	20th Century-Fox
	Show Them No Mercy	20th Century-Fox
1936	*Everybody's Old Man*	20th Century-Fox
	Pigskin Parade	20th Century-Fox
1937	*Love Is News*	20th Century-Fox
	Nancy Steele Is Missing	20th Century-Fox
	Fifty Roads to Town	20th Century-Fox
	You Can't Have Everything	20th Century-Fox
	(O, A: Buttolph, Scharf, Virgil, Mockridge, Spencer, Prima, Rose, Maxwell)	
	Danger—Love at Work	20th Century-Fox
	Second Honeymoon	20th Century-Fox
1938	*Josette*	20th Century-Fox

---

* Two scores were written for this film. Carli D. Elinor composed
the first one, Breil the second.

1939	*The Three Musketeers* (PS: Maxwell)	20th Century-Fox
	Wife, Husband and Friend (PS: Maxwell)	20th Century-Fox
	The Gorilla	20th Century-Fox
	Hotel for Women	20th Century-Fox
	Barricade	20th Century-Fox
1940	*He Married His Wife*	20th Century-Fox
	Star Dust	20th Century-Fox
	I Was an Adventuress	20th Century-Fox
	Four Sons	20th Century-Fox
	The Man I Married	20th Century-Fox
	The Return of Frank James	20th Century-Fox
1941	*Western Union*	20th Century-Fox
	Tobacco Road	20th Century-Fox
	Confirm or Deny	20th Century-Fox

SCORE:

1940	*Chad Hanna*	20th Century-Fox
1941	*Swamp Water*	20th Century-Fox
	Bahama Passage	Paramount
1942	*Lady for a Night*	Republic
	My Favorite Blonde	Paramount
	This Gun for Hire	Paramount
	Moontide (with Mockridge)	20th
	In Old California	Republic
	Wake Island	Paramount
	Manila Calling (with Mockridge, Raksin)	20th
	Thunder Birds	20th
	Street of Chance	Paramount
1943	*Immortal Sergeant*	20th
	Crash Dive (O: De Packh)	20th
	Bomber's Moon	20th
	Corvette K-225	Universal
	Guadalcanal Diary	20th
1944	*Buffalo Bill*	20th
	The Hitler Gang	Paramount
	Till We Meet Again	Paramount
	In the Meantime, Darling	20th
1945	*The Fighting Lady* (doc.; O: De Packh)	20th
	Circumstantial Evidence (O: De Packh)	20th
	The Bullfighters	20th
	Nob Hill (O: Rose)	20th
	Within These Walls (O: A. Morton)	20th
	Junior Miss (O: De Packh)	20th
	The Caribbean Mystery (O: Cutner)	20th

	The House on 92nd Street	20th
	The Spider	20th
1946	*Shock* (O: A. Morton)	20th
	Johnny Comes Flying Home (O: A. Morton)	20th
	Somewhere in the Night (O: A. Morton)	20th
	Strange Triangle (O: A. Morton)	20th
	It Shouldn't Happen to a Dog (O: A. Morton)	20th
	Home Sweet Homicide (O: De Packh)	20th
1947	*13 Rue Madeleine* (O: Cutner, Powell, Shuken)	20th
	Boomerang (O: Powell)	20th
	The Brasher Doubloon (O: De Packh)	20th
	Moss Rose (O: De Packh, Powell)	20th
	Kiss of Death (O: Hagen)	20th
	The Foxes of Harrow (O: De Packh)	20th
1948	*Bill and Coo* (O: Cutner, Shuken)	Republic
	To the Victor (O: Raab)	WB
	Smart Girls Don't Talk (O: Raab)	WB
	June Bride (O: Cutner, Shuken)	WB
1949	*John Loves Mary* (O: Raab)	WB
	Colorado Territory (O: Cutner, de Packh, Shuken)	WB
	The Girl from Jones Beach (O: Cutner, Raab)	WB
	One Last Fling (O: Raab)	WB
	Roseanna McCoy (O: Moross)	Goldwyn-RKO
	The Story of Seabiscuit (O: De Packh)	WB
1950	*Montana* (O: Cutner, Shuken)	WB
	Chain Lightning (O: De Packh)	WB
	Return of the Frontiersman (O: De Packh)	WB
	Pretty Baby (O: De Packh)	WB
	Three Secrets (O: De Packh)	WB
1951	*The Enforcer* (O: De Packh)	WB
	The Redhead and the Cowboy	Paramount
	Fighting Coast Guard	Republic
	Along the Great Divide (O: De Packh)	WB
	Fort Worth	WB
	Submarine Command	Paramount
	Ten Tall Men	Norma-Col
1952	*The Sellout*	MGM
	Lone Star	MGM
	This Woman Is Dangerous (O: De Packh)	WB
	Talk About a Stranger	MGM
	Carson City (O: Cutner, Shuken)	WB
	The Winning Team (O: De Packh)	WB
	My Man and I	MGM
1953	*The Man Behind the Gun*	WB

1945	*Utah*	Republic
	Flame of Barbary Coast	Republic
	Man from Oklahoma	Republic
	Tell It to a Star	Republic
	Sunset in El Dorado	Republic
	Don't Fence Me In	Republic
	An Angel Comes to Brooklyn	Republic
	Along the Navajo Trail	Republic
1946	*Gay Blades*	Republic
	Song of Arizona (O: Glickman, Kahn)	Republic
	Home on the Range	Republic
	The Catman of Paris (O: Maxwell)	Republic
	Rainbow Over Texas	Republic
	One Exciting Week	Republic
	My Pal Trigger (O: Kahn)	Republic
	Night Train to Memphis	Republic
	Under Nevada Skies	Republic
	Roll On Texas Moon	Republic
	Affairs of Geraldine	Republic
	Sioux City Sue	Republic
	Heldorado	Republic
1947	*The Crimson Key*	Wurtzel-20th
	Second Chance	Wurtzel-20th
	The Invisible Wall	Wurtzel-20th
1948	*Eyes of Texas*	Republic
	Night Time in Nevada	Republic
	Son of God's Country	Republic
	The Denver Kid	Republic
	The Plunderers	Republic
	The Far Frontier	Republic
1949	*The Last Bandit* (O: Wilson)	Republic
	Hellfire (O: Wilson)	Republic
	Too Late for Tears	Stromberg-UA
	Down Dakota Way (O: Wilson)	Republic
1950	*Bells of Coronado* (O: Wilson)	Republic
	Women from Headquarters (O: Scott, Wilson)	Republic
	Rock Island Trail (O: Wilson)	Republic
	The Savage Horde (O: Wilson)	Republic
	Trigger, Jr. (O: Scott, Wilson)	Republic
	Sunset in the West	Republic
	Hit Parade of 1951 (O: Wilson)	Republic
	North of the Great Divide	Republic
1951	*Spoilers of the Plains*	Republic
	Oh! Susanna	Republic
	Heart of the Rockies	Republic

10

BUTTS *(Continued)*

	In Old Amarillo	Republic
	South of Caliente	Republic
	The Sea Hornet	Republic
1952	*Colorado Sundown*	Republic
	Bal Tabarin	Republic
	Woman of the North Country	Republic
	Toughest Man in Arizona	Republic
	The WAC from Walla Walla	Republic

HAROLD BYRNS

1951	*Pickup*	Forum-Columbia
	The Girl on the Bridge	Forum-20th

EMIL CADKIN

1947	*Three on a Ticket*	PRC
	The Big Fix	PRC
	Heartaches	PRC
	Bury Me Dead	PRC

CHARLES WAKEFIELD CADMAN

1930	*Captain of the Guard*	Universal

JOHN CAGE

	Horror Dream	Peterson
1948	*Dreams That Money Can Buy*	Films Intl. of America
	(with Applebaum, Bowles, Diamond, Milhaud)	
1950	*Works of Calder*	Herbert Matter

LUCIEN CAILLIET

1945	*The Enchanted Forest* (with Malotte)	PRC
1947	*Fun on a Weekend*	Stone-UA
1948	*The Winner's Circle*	Polimer-20th
	Harpoon	Danches-SG
	Thunder in the Pines	Lippert-SG
	Trouble Preferred	Wurtzel-20th
	State Department—File 649	Neufeld-FC

11

1949	*Red Stallion in the Rockies*	Eagle Lion
	Special Agent	Pine-Thomas-Par
1950	*Captain China*	Pine-Thomas-Par
	Tripoli	Pine-Thomas-Par
1951	*The Last Outpost*	Pine-Thomas-Par
	Crosswinds	Pine-Thomas-Par
1952	*Hong Kong*	Pine-Thomas-Par
	Confidence Girl	Stone-UA
	Caribbean	Pine-Thomas-Par
	The Blazing Forest	Pine-Thomas-Par
1953	*Tropic Zone*	Pine-Thomas-Par
	The Conquerors	Pine-Thomas-Par

DARRELL CALKER

1946	*Rolling Home*	Lippert-SG
	Dangerous Millions	Wurtzel-20th
	Renegade Girl	Affiliated-SG
1947	*Backlash*	Wurtzel-20th
	Shoot to Kill	Screen Guild
	Big Town	Pine-Thomas-Par
	Jewels of Brandenburg	Wurtzel-20th
	I Cover Big Town	Pine-Thomas-Par
	Adventure Island	Pine-Thomas-Par
1948	*Albuquerque*	Pine-Thomas-Par
	Half Past Midnight	Wurtzel-20th
	Silent Conflict	Cassidy-UA
	Arthur Takes Over	Wurtzel-20th
	Speed to Spare	Pine-Thomas-Par
	Big Town Scandal	Pine-Thomas-Par
	Fighting Back	Wurtzel-20th
1949	*Dynamite*	Pine-Thomas-Par
	Ride, Ryder, Ride	Equity-EL
	El Paso	Pine-Thomas-Par
	Tucson	Wurtzel-20th
	Manhandled	Pine-Thomas-Par
1950	*The Flying Saucer*	Colonial-FC
	Federal Man	Schwarz-EL
	I Killed Geronimo	Schwarz-EL
	The Fighting Redhead	Equity-EL
1951	*The Hoodlum*	Schwarz-UA
	Savage Drums	Lippert
	Cattle Queen	United Intl.-UA
	Joe Palooka in Triple Cross	Monogram

Slaughter Trail (MD)	Allen-RKO
F. B. I. Girl	Lippert
Superman and the Mole Men	Lippert

GERARD CARBONARA

SCORE:

1928	*Warming Up*	Paramount
	Sawdust Paradise	Paramount
	The Patriot (with Domenico Savino)	Paramount
1932	*Traffic* (short)	Educational
	Any Way to Get There (short)	Educational
	On the Farm (short)	Educational
	Across America (short)	Educational
1935	*The Promised Land* (doc.)	Zionist Society
1936	*The Trail of the Lonesome Pine*	Paramount
	Fatal Lady (with Young)	Paramount
	Girl of the Ozarks	Paramount
	The Texas Rangers (A: Roder)	Paramount
1938	*The Texans*	Paramount
	The Arkansas Traveler	Paramount
	Mysterious Rider	Paramount
	Men with Wings (with Harling; A: Cailliet)	Paramount
	Tom Sawyer, Detective	Paramount
1939	*The Gracie Allen Murder Case*	Paramount
	Our Leading Citizen	Paramount
1940	*Geronimo* (with Leipold)	Paramount
	Parole Fixer	Paramount
	Women Without Names	Paramount
	Dr. Cyclops (with Toch, Malotte)	Paramount
	Island of Doomed Men	Columbia
	I Married Adventure	Columbia
1941	*The Round-Up*	Paramount
	The Shepherd of the Hills	Paramount
	The Night of January 16th	Paramount
	Among the Living	Paramount
1942	*Pacific Blackout*	Paramount
	Tombstone	Paramount
	American Empire	Sherman-UA
1943	*Night Plane from Chungking*	Paramount
	The Kansan	Sherman-UA
	Henry Aldrich Haunts a House	Paramount
1944	*Easy Money* (short)	MGM
	By Your Command (short)	MGM
	The Immortal Blacksmith (short)	MGM

	The Town Went Wild	PRC
1945	*Clean Waters* (short)	Raphael G. Wolff
	Welding (short)	Raphael G. Wolff
	Transportation (short)	Raphael G. Wolff
	Transit (short)	Raphael G. Wolff
1946	*Running Water on the Farm* (short)	Raphael G. Wolff
	More Power to the American Farmer (short)	Raphael G. Wolff
	More Power to America (short)	Raphael G. Wolff
1947	*Of This We Are Proud* (short)	Raphael G. Wolff
1948	*"By Their Works"* (short)	Raphael G. Wolff
	Textile Industry (short)	Raphael G. Wolff
	Highway Highlights (short)	Raphael G. Wolff

PARTIAL SCORE:

1936	*Big Brown Eyes*	Paramount
	The Moon's Our Home	Paramount
	The Sky Parade	Paramount
	The Case Against Mrs. Ames	Paramount
	Forgotten Faces	Paramount
	Palm Springs	Paramount
	Poppy	Paramount
	Spendthrift	Paramount
	Wedding Present	Paramount
1938	*Arrest Bulldog Drummond*	Paramount
	Sunset Trail	Paramount
	Escape from Yesterday	Paramount
	Artists and Models Abroad	Paramount
1939	*Disbarred*	Paramount
	Ambush	Paramount
	Paris Honeymoon (with Shuken)	Paramount
	King of Chinatown	Paramount
1946	*Abilene Town* (with Terr; O: Koff)	Levey-UA
1949	*The Big Wheel* (with Leipold, Finston)	Popkin-UA

MARIO CASTELNUOVO-TEDESCO

1943	*The Return of the Vampire*	Columbia
1944	*Two-Man Submarine*	Columbia
	The Black Parachute	Columbia
	She's a Soldier Too	Columbia
1945	*I Love a Mystery*	Columbia
	The Crime Doctor's Courage	Columbia
	And Then There Were None	Popular-20th
	Prison Ship	Columbia

CASTELNUOVO-TEDESCO *(Continued)*

1946	*Night Editor*	Columbia
	Dangerous Business	Columbia
1947	*Time Out of Mind* (with Rozsa)	UI
	(O: Cutner, Shuken, Zador)	
1948	*The Loves of Carmen*	Columbia
1951	*Mask of the Avenger*	Columbia
1952	*The Brigand*	Columbia

CHARLES CHAPLIN

1925	*The Gold Rush* (with Elinor)	Chaplin-UA
1931	*City Lights* (A: Arthur Johnston)	Chaplin-UA
1936	*Modern Times* (A: D. Raksin)	Chaplin-UA
1940	*The Great Dictator* (with Willson)	Chaplin-UA
1942	*The Gold Rush* (reissue; with Terr, Carbonara)	Chaplin-UA
1947	*Monsieur Verdoux* (A: Schrager)	Chaplin-UA
1952	*Limelight* (A: Ray Rasch)	Chaplin-UA

FRANK CHURCHILL

1938	*Snow White and the Seven Dwarfs*	Disney-RKO
	(with Harline, Smith)	
1941	*The Reluctant Dragon*	Disney-RKO
	Dumbo (with Wallace; O: Plumb)	Disney-RKO
1942	*Bambi* (with Plumb; O: Smith, Wolcott)	Disney-RKO

ANTHONY COLLINS

1937	*Victoria the Great*	Wilcox-RKO
1938	*The Rat*	Wilcox-RKO
	Sixty Glorious Years	Wilcox-RKO
	A Royal Divorce	Wilcox-Par
1939	*Nurse Edith Cavell*	Wilcox-RKO
	Allegheny Uprising	RKO
1940	*Swiss Family Robinson*	RKO
	Irene (MD; O: Collins, Rose)	Wilcox-RKO
	Tom Brown's School Days	RKO
	No, No, Nanette (MD)	Wilcox-RKO
1941	*Sunny* (MD; O: Collins, Rose)	Wilcox-RKO
	Unexpected Uncle	RKO
1943	*Forever and a Day*	U.N.-RKO
	Destroyer	Columbia
1946	*A Yank in London*	Wilcox-20th

15

	Piccadilly Incident	Wilcox
1947	*The Fabulous Texan*	Republic
	The Courtneys of Curzon Street	Wilcox
1951	*Odette*	Wilcox-UA
	The Lady with the Lamp	Wilcox
1952	*Macao*	RKO
	Trent's Last Case	Wilcox

ALBERTO COLOMBO

1933	*Million Dollar Melody* (short)	Educational
1934.	*Red Morning*	RKO
1935	*Romance in Manhattan*	RKO
	Grand Old Girl	RKO
	Murder on a Honeymoon	RKO
	A Dog of Flanders	RKO
	Chasing Yesterday	RKO
	Village Tale	RKO
	Hooray for Love	RKO
	Jalna	RKO
	Hot Tip	RKO
	The Return of Peter Grimm	RKO
	His Family Tree	RKO
	Powder Smoke Range	RKO
	Freckles	RKO
	To Beat the Band	RKO
	Annie Oakley	RKO
	Seven Keys to Baldpate	RKO
1936	*Two in the Dark*	RKO
	Chatterbox	RKO
	Love on a Bet	RKO
	Yellow Dust	RKO
	The Farmer in the Dell	RKO
	Two in Revolt	RKO
	The Last Outlaw	RKO
	M'liss	RKO
	Grand Jury	RKO
1937	*The Hit Parade*	Republic
	Michael O'Halloran	Republic
	The Affairs of Cappy Ricks	Republic
	Dangerous Holiday	Republic
	Rhythm in the Clouds	Republic
	It Could Happen to You	Republic
	Meet the Boy Friend	Republic

	Sea Racketeers	Republic
	The Sheik Steps Out	Republic
	All Over Town	Republic
	Escape by Night	Republic
	Youth on Parole	Republic
	The Wrong Road	Republic
	Portia on Trial	Republic
	Manhattan Merry-Go-Round	Republic
	Springtime in the Rockies	Republic
	Zorro Rides Again (serial)	Republic
	The Duke Comes Back	Republic
	Wild Horse Rodeo	Republic
	Exiled to Shanghai	Republic
1938	*Lady, Behave!*	Republic
	Mama Runs Wild	Republic
	The Purple Vigilantes	Republic
	The Old Barn Dance	Republic
	Outside of Paradise	Republic
	The Lone Ranger (serial)	Republic
	Born to Be Wild	Republic
	Hollywood Stadium Mystery	Republic
	Prison Nurse	Republic
	Call the Mesquiteers	Republic
	King of the Newsboys	Republic
	Arson Gang Busters	Republic
	Invisible Enemy	Republic
	Outlaws of Sonora	Republic
	Call of the Yukon	Republic
	Under Western Stars	Republic
	Romance on the Run	Republic
	Gangs of New York	Republic
	The Fighting Devil Dogs (serial)	Republic
	Ladies in Distress	Republic
	Gold Mine in the Sky	Republic
1949	*The Sickle or the Cross*	Roland Reed
1950	*The Sundowners*	Lemay-Templeton-EL
	Black Hand	MGM
	Messenger of Peace	Roland Reed
1951	*Go for Broke!* (AC: Cutner, Shuken)	MGM
	All That I Have	Family Films
1952	*Holiday for Sinners* (MD)	MGM
	You for Me (MD)	MGM
	Apache War Smoke (MD)	MGM
1953	*Rogue's March*	MGM

17

AARON COPLAND

1939	*The City* (documentary)	Civic Films
1940	*Of Mice and Men*	Roach-UA
	Our Town	Lesser-UA
1943	*The North Star*	Goldwyn-RKO
1945	*The Cummington Story* (documentary)	O.W.I.
1949	*The Red Pony*	Republic
	The Heiress (O: Van Cleave)	Paramount

SIDNEY CUTNER

SCORE:

1938	*Holiday*	Columbia
1940	*His Girl Friday*	Columbia

COMPOSITION & ORCHESTRATION:

1938	*City Streets*	Columbia
	The Lady Objects	Columbia
	Flight to Fame	Columbia
1939	*Homicide Bureau*	Columbia
1940	*Music in My Heart*	Columbia
	The Lone Wolf Strikes	Columbia
	The Lone Wolf Meets a Lady	Columbia
	The Lone Wolf Keeps a Date	Columbia
1941	*The Face Behind the Mask*	Columbia
	The Lone Wolf Takes a Chance	Columbia
	Texas	Columbia
1949	*The Best Years* (Anniversary Trailer; with Shuken)	MGM

LOUIS DE FRANCESCO

1932	*Chandu the Magician*	Fox
1933	*State Fair*	Fox
	Pleasure Cruise	Fox
	Cavalcade	Fox
	I Loved You Wednesday	Fox
	The Power and the Glory	Fox
	Berkeley Square	Fox
	Hoopla	Fox
	Mr. Skitch	Fox
	As Husbands Go	Fox
1934	*Carolina*	Fox
	David Harum	Fox
	Coming Out Party	Fox

DE FRANCESCO *(Continued)*

	All Men Are Enemies	Fox
	Such Women Are Dangerous	Fox
	Change of Heart	Fox
	Springtime for Henry	Fox
	The World Moves On	Fox
	Grand Canary	Fox
	The White Parade	Fox
	Helldorado	Fox
1935	*The Gay Deception*	Fox
	Here's to Romance	Fox
1940	*The Ramparts We Watch*	March of Time-RKO
	(with Jacques Dallin, Peter Brunelli)	
1942	*United We Stand*	20th Century-Fox

1940-1949 Composed music for 105 short subjects for 20th Century-Fox Movietone, N. Y., and for Movietone News.

RUDY DE SAXE

1947	*Bells of San Fernando*	Screen Guild
	Beyond Our Own	Religious Film Assoc.
1950	*The Texan Meets Calamity Jane*	Lamb-Col

PAUL DESSAU

1946	*Combat Fatigue* (documentary)	U. S. Navy
	The Wife of Monte Cristo	PRC
1947	*Winter Wonderland* (AC, O: Law)	Republic
	The Pretender	Republic
1948	*Devil's Cargo*	Falcon-FC
	The Vicious Circle	Wilder-UA

ADOLPH DEUTSCH

ORCHESTRAL ARRANGEMENTS:

1938	*Fools for Scandal*	WB
	Cowboy from Brooklyn	WB

SCORE:

1937	*Mr. Dodd Takes the Air*	WB
	They Won't Forget	WB
	The Great Garrick (O: Friedhofer)	WB
1938	*Swing Your Lady*	WB

19

	Racket Busters	WB
	Valley of the Giants (with Friedhofer)	WB
	Heart of the North	WB
1939	*Off the Record*	WB
	The Kid from Kokomo	WB
	Indianapolis Speedway	WB
	Angels Wash Their Faces	WB
	Espionage Agent	WB
1940	*The Fighting 69th* (O: Friedhofer)	WB
	Castle on the Hudson	WB
	Three Cheers for the Irish	WB
	Saturday's Children	WB
	Torrid Zone	WB
	They Drive by Night	WB
	Flowing Gold	WB
	Tugboat Annie Sails Again	WB
	East of the River	WB
1941	*High Sierra*	WB
	The Great Mr. Nobody	WB
	Singapore Woman	WB
	Underground	WB
	Kisses for Breakfast	WB
	Manpower	WB
	The Maltese Falcon	WB
1942	*All Through the Night*	WB
	Larceny, Inc.	WB
	Juke Girl	WB
	The Big Shot	WB
	Across the Pacific	WB
	You Can't Escape Forever	WB
	George Washington Slept Here	WB
	Lucky Jordan	Paramount
1943	*Action in the North Atlantic* (O: Moross)	WB
	Northern Pursuit (O: Moross)	WB
1944	*Uncertain Glory* (O: Moross)	WB
	The Mask of Dimitrios (O: Moross)	WB
	The Doughgirls	WB
1945	*Escape in the Desert* (O: Moross)	WB
	Danger Signal (O: Cutter)	WB
1946	*Three Strangers* (O: Moross)	WB
	Shadow of a Woman (O: Cutter)	WB
	Nobody Lives Forever (O: Moross, Burke)	WB
1947	*Ramrod*	Enterprise-UA
	Blaze of Noon (O: Cutner, Shuken)	Paramount
1948	*Julia Misbehaves*	MGM

1949	*Whispering Smith* (O: Cutner, Shuken)	Paramount
	Little Women	MGM
	The Stratton Story	MGM
	Intruder in the Dust	MGM
1950	*Stars in My Crown*	MGM
	The Big Hangover	MGM
	Father of the Bride (O: Courage, Heglin)	MGM
	Mrs. O'Malley and Mr. Malone	MGM
1951	*Soldiers Three*	MGM

MUSICAL DIRECTION:

1949	*Take Me Out to the Ball Game*	MGM
1950	*Annie Get Your Gun* (O: Courage, de Packh, Franklyn, Hagen, Marquardt, Salinger)	MGM
	Pagan Love Song (O: Franklyn, Salinger)	MGM
1951	*Show Boat* (O: Salinger, Courage)	MGM
1952	*The Belle of New York* (O: De Packh, Salinger)	MGM
	Million Dollar Mermaid (O: Courage)	MGM

DAVID DIAMOND

1940	*A Place to Live* (doc.)	Philadelphia Housing Assoc.
1948	*Dreams That Money Can Buy*	Films Intl. of America
	(with Applebaum, Bowles, Cage, Milhaud)	
	Strange Victory (documentary)	Target
1949	*Anna Lucasta*	Security-Columbia

ROBERT EMMETT DOLAN

SCORE:

1942	*Are Husbands Necessary?*	Paramount
	The Major and the Minor	Paramount
	Once Upon a Honeymoon	RKO
1944	*Standing Room Only*	Paramount
	Lady in the Dark (O: Bennett)	Paramount
	I Love a Soldier	Paramount
1945	*Salty O'Rourke*	Paramount
	Murder, He Says	Paramount
	The Bells of St. Mary's	Rainbow-RKO
1946	*Monsieur Beaucaire* (O: Hallenbeck)	Paramount
1947	*Cross My Heart*	Paramount
	My Favorite Brunette	Paramount
	Welcome Stranger	Paramount

21

	The Trouble with Women (with Young)	Paramount
	(O: Cutner, Shuken)	
	The Perils of Pauline (O: Hallenbeck)	Paramount
	Dear Ruth	Paramount
1948	*Saigon*	Paramount
	Mr. Peabody and the Mermaid	UI
	Good Sam	Rainbow-RKO
1949	*My Own True Love* (O: Cutner, Shuken)	Paramount
	Sorrowful Jones	Paramount
	The Great Gatsby (O: Cutner, Shuken)	Paramount
1952	*My Son John*	Paramount

MUSICAL DIRECTION:

1941	*Birth of the Blues*	Paramount
	Louisiana Purchase (A: Scharf)	Paramount
1942	*Holiday Inn* (A: Scharf)	Paramount
1943	*Star Spangled Rhythm*	Paramount
	Happy Go Lucky	Paramount
	Dixie	Paramount
1944	*Going My Way*	Paramount
	Here Come the Waves	Paramount
1945	*Bring On the Girls*	Paramount
	Incendiary Blonde	Paramount
	Duffy's Tavern	Paramount
	The Stork Club	Paramount
1946	*Blue Skies*	Paramount
1947	*Road to Rio*	Paramount
1949	*Top o' the Morning* (O: Van Cleave)	Paramount
1950	*Let's Dance* (O: Cutner, Shuken, Van Cleave)	Paramount
1952	*Aaron Slick from Punkin Crick*	Paramount
	(O: Cutner, Shuken)	

CARMEN DRAGON

ORCHESTRATION:
1944	*Cover Girl*	Columbia

SCORE:
1944	*Mr. Winkle Goes to War*	Columbia
	(with Sawtell; O: Cutner)	
1946	*Young Widow* (O: Hallenbeck)	Stromberg-UA
	The Strange Woman	Stromberg-UA
1947	*Dishonored Lady*	Stromberg-UA
	Out of the Blue	Eagle Lion

1948	*The Time of Your Life*	Cagney-UA
1950	*Kiss Tomorrow Goodbye*	Cagney-WB
1951	*Night Into Morning*	MGM
	The Law and the Lady	MGM
	The People Against O'Hara	MGM
1952	*When in Rome*	MGM

MUSICAL DIRECTION:

1946	*The Kid from Brooklyn*	Goldwyn-RKO
1952	*Lovely to Look At* (with S. Chaplin; O: Arnaud)	MGM

JOSEPH DUBIN

1944	*Tucson Raiders*	Republic
	The Tiger Woman (serial)	Republic
	Marshal of Reno	Republic
	Call of the Rockies	Republic
	Silver City Kid	Republic
	Bordertown Trail	Republic
	The San Antonio Kid	Republic
	Haunted Harbor (serial)	Republic
	Stagecoach to Monterey	Republic
	Cheyenne Wildcat	Republic
	Code of the Prairie	Republic
	Sheriff of Sundown	Repulbic
	Vigilantes of Dodge City	Republic
	Firebrands of Arizona	Republic
1945	*Bells of Rosarita*	Republic
	Girls of the Big House	Republic
1946	*The Madonna's Secret* (O: Glickman)	Republic
	Rendezvous with Annie	Republic
	Home in Oklahoma	Republic
1947	*Trail to San Antone*	Republic
	The Ghost Goes Wild (O: Scott)	Republic
1950	*Bee at the Beach* (cartoon)	Disney-RKO
	Chicken in the Rough (cartoon)	Disney-RKO
	Cold Storage (cartoon)	Disney-RKO
	Plutopia (cartoon)	Disney-RKO
	If You Don't Watch Out (documentary)	

GEORGE DUNING

MUSICAL ARRANGEMENTS:

1939	*That's Right, You're Wrong*	RKO

1940	*You'll Find Out*	RKO
1941	*Playmates*	RKO
1942	*My Favorite Spy*	RKO
1943	*Around the World*	RKO

ORCHESTRATIONS:

1944	*Carolina Blues*	Columbia
1945	*Let's Go Steady*	Columbia
	Eadie Was a Lady	Columbia

MUSICAL DIRECTION:

1946	*Sing While You Dance*	Columbia
	Singin' in the Corn	Columbia
1951	*Sunny Side of the Street*	Columbia
1952	*Affair in Trinidad*	Columbia
	Rainbow 'Round My Shoulder	Columbia

SCORE:

(Orchestrations by Arthur Morton unless otherwise indicated)

1947	*Johnny O'Clock*	Columbia
	The Guilt of Janet Ames	Columbia
	The Corpse Came C.O.D.	Columbia
	Down to Earth (with Roemheld; Greek ballet	Columbia
	music: Castelnuovo-Tedesco; O: Hagen, Gilbert)	
	Her Husband's Affairs	Columbia
1948	*I Love Trouble*	Columbia
	To the Ends of the Earth	Columbia
	The Untamed Breed	Columbia
	The Return of October	Columbia
	The Gallant Blade	Columbia
	The Man from Colorado	Columbia
1949	*Shockproof*	Columbia
	The Dark Past (O: Gilbert)	Columbia
	Slightly French	Columbia
	The Undercover Man	Columbia
	Lust for Gold	Columbia
	Johnny Allegro	Columbia
	The Doolins of Oklahoma (with Sawtell)	Columbia
	Jolson Sings Again (O: L. Russell)	Columbia
	And Baby Makes Three	Columbia
1950	*Cargo to Capetown*	Columbia
	No Sad Songs for Me	Columbia
	Convicted	Columbia
	The Petty Girl	Columbia
	Between Midnight and Dawn	Columbia

	Harriet Craig	Columbia
1951	*The Flying Missile*	Columbia
	Lorna Doone	Columbia
	Two of a Kind	Columbia
	The Lady and the Bandit	Columbia
	The Mob	Columbia
	The Barefoot Mailman	Columbia
	The Family Secret	Columbia
	Man in the Saddle	Columbia
1952	*Scandal Sheet*	Columbia
	Sound Off	Columbia
	Paula	Columbia
	Captain Pirate	Columbia
	Assignment—Paris	Columbia
1953	*Last of the Comanches*	Columbia
	All Ashore (A: Nelson Riddle)	Columbia
	Salome (music for dances: Amfitheatrof)	Columbia

PAUL DUNLAP

1950	*The Baron of Arizona*	Lippert
	Hi-Jacked	Lippert
1951	*The Steel Helmet*	Lippert
	Cry Danger	Olympic-RKO
	Little Big Horn	Lippert
	Lost Continent	Lippert
	Journey Into Light	Bernhard-20th
1952	*The San Francisco Story*	Fidelity-Vogue-WB
	Breakdown	Pegasus-Realart
	Park Row	Fuller-UA
	Big Jim McLain	Wayne-Fellows-WB
	Hellgate	Commander-Lippert

HANNS EISLER

1939	*The 400 Million*	Ivens-Garrison
	Pete Roleum and His Cousins	Joseph Losey
	Soil	Dept. of Agriculture
1940	*White Floods*	Frontier Films
	Rain	Joris Ivens
1941	*The Forgotten Village*	Herbert Kline
1943	*Hangmen Also Die*	Pressburger-UA
1944	*None But the Lonely Heart*	RKO

EISLER *(Continued)*

1945	*Jealousy*	Republic
	The Spanish Main	RKO
1946	*Deadline at Dawn*	RKO
	A Scandal in Paris (O: Byrns)	Pressburger-UA
1947	*The Woman on the Beach* (O: Grau)	RKO
1948	*So Well Remembered*	RKO

CARLI D. ELINOR

SCORE ADAPTED, COMPOSED, AND ARRANGED:

1915	*The Birth of a Nation**	Griffith
1918	*Hearts of the World*	Griffith
1925	*The Gold Rush* (with Chaplin)	Chaplin-UA
1926	*What Price Glory?* (with Bassett; O: Baron)	Fox
1927	*Seventh Heaven* (with Bassett)	Fox
1929	*The Bridge of San Luis Rey*	MGM

LEO ERDODY

1942	*Baby Face Morgan*	PRC
	Tomorrow We Live	PRC
	City of Silent Men	PRC
1943	*Dead Men Walk*	PRC
	Queen of Broadway	PRC
	Corregidor	PRC
	My Son, the Hero	PRC
	Wild Horse Rustlers	PRC
	Girls in Chains	PRC
	Isle of Forgotten Sins	PRC
	Fugitive of the Plains	PRC
1944	*Bluebeard*	PRC
1945	*Strange Illusion*	PRC
	Apology for Murder	PRC
	White Pongo	PRC
	Detour	PRC
1946	*The Flying Serpent*	PRC
	I Ring Doorbells	PRC
	Murder Is My Business	PRC
	Larceny in Her Heart	PRC
	Blonde for a Day	PRC
	Gas House Kids	PRC
1947	*The Return of Rin Tin Tin*	Romay-EL

* See note on this film under Briel.

	Blonde Savage	Ensign-EL
1948	*Money Madness*	Neufeld-FC
	Lady at Midnight	Sutherland-EL

CY FEUER

1938	*Pals of the Saddle*	Republic
	The Higgins Family	Republic
	Billy the Kid Returns	Republic
	The Night Hawk	Republic
	Down in 'Arkansaw' (A: Torbett)	Republic
	I Stand Accused	Republic
	Storm Over Bengal	Republic
	Come On, Rangers	Republic
	Orphans of the Street	Republic
	Shine On Harvest Moon	Republic
	Federal Man-Hunt	Republic
1939	*Fighting Thoroughbreds*	Republic
	The Mysterious Miss X	Republic
	Pride of the Navy	Republic
	Woman Doctor	Republic
	Forged Passport	Republic
	I Was a Convict	Republic
	Rough Riders Round-Up	Republic
	Frontier Pony Express	Republic
	Street of Missing Men	Republic
	Southward Ho!	Republic
	My Wife's Relatives	Republic
	The Zero Hour	Republic
	S.O.S.—Tidal Wave	Republic
	In Old Caliente	Republic
	Mickey, the Kid	Republic
	She Married a Cop	Republic
	Should Husbands Work?	Republic
	Smuggled Cargo	Republic
	Flight at Midnight	Republic
	Wall Street Cowboy	Republic
	Calling All Marines	Republic
	The Arizona Kid	Republic
	Sabotage	Republic
	Jeepers Creepers	Republic
	Main Street Lawyer	Republic
	The Covered Trailer	Republic
	Saga of Death Valley	Republic
	Days of Jesse James	Republic

	Thou Shalt Not Kill	Republic
	Money to Burn	Republic
1940	*Heroes of the Saddle*	Republic
	Wolf of New York	Republic
	Village Barn Dance	Republic
	Pioneers of the West	Republic
	Forgotten Girls	Republic
	Ghost Valley Raiders	Republic
	In Old Missouri	Republic
	Grandpa Goes to Town	Republic
	Covered Wagon Days	Republic
	The Crooked Road	Republic
	Gangs of Chicago	Republic
	Rocky Mountain Rangers	Republic
	Women in War	Republic
	Wagons Westward	Republic
	Grand Ole Opry	Republic
	One Man's Law	Republic
	The Carson City Kid	Republic
	Scatterbrain	Republic
	Girl from God's Country	Republic
	The Ranger and the Lady	Republic
	Sing, Dance, Plenty Hot	Republic
	The Tulsa Kid	Republic
	Earl of Puddlestone	Republic
	Girl from Havana	Republic
	Colorado	Republic
	Under Texas Skies	Republic
	Frontier Vengeance	Republic
	Melody and Moonlight	Republic
	Hit Parade of 1941 (O: Rose, Scharf)	Republic
	Young Bill Hickok	Republic
	Who Killed Aunt Maggie?	Republic
	Friendly Neighbors	Republic
	The Trail Blazers	Republic
	Meet the Missus	Republic
	The Border Legion	Republic
	Barnyard Follies	Republic
	Behind the News	Republic
	Lone Star Raiders	Republic
	Bowery Boy	Republic
	The Mysterious Dr. Satan (serial)	Republic
1941	*Wyoming Wildcat*	Republic
	Robin Hood of the Pecos	Republic
	Arkansas Judge	Republic
	Petticoat Politics	Republic

The Phantom Cowboy	Republic
Prairie Pioneers	Republic
A Man Betrayed	Republic
The Great Train Robbery	Republic
Mr. District Attorney	Republic
In Old Cheyenne	Republic
Two Gun Sheriff	Republic
Sis Hopkins (O: Scharf)	Republic
Rookies on Parade (O: Rose, Scharf)	Republic
Lady from Louisiana	Republic
Sheriff of Tombstone	Republic
The Gay Vagabond	Republic
Desert Bandit	Republic
Saddlemates	Republic
Angels with Broken Wings	Republic
Nevada City	Republic
Kansas Cyclone	Republic
Puddin' Head (O: Scharf)	Republic
Mountain Moonlight	Republic
Hurricane Smith	Republic
Citadel of Crime	Republic
Rags to Riches	Republic
Ice-Capades	Republic
Doctors Don't Tell	Republic
The Pittsburgh Kid	Republic
Bad Man of Deadwood	Republic
Outlaws of the Cherokee Trail	Republic
The Apache Kid	Republic
Death Valley Outlaws	Republic
Sailors on Leave	Republic
Mercy Island	Republic
Jesse James at Bay	Republic
Gauchos of Eldorado	Republic
Public Enemies	Republic
The Devil Pays Off	Republic
Tuxedo Junction	Republic
Red River Valley	Republic
West of Cimarron	Republic
Mr. District Attorney in the Carter Case	Republic
Adventures of Captain Marvel (serial)	Republic
1942 *Arizona Terrors*	Republic
Man from Cheyenne	Republic
Pardon My Stripes	Republic
Code of the Outlaw	Republic
A Tragedy at Midnight	Republic
South of Santa Fe	Republic

29

	Sleepytime Gal (O: Rose)	Republic
	Stagecoach Express	Republic
	Yokel Boy (O: Rose)	Republic
	Raiders of the Range	Republic
	Affairs of Jimmy Valentine	Republic
	Jesse James, Jr.	Republic
	Shepherd of the Ozarks	Republic
	Sunset on the Desert	Republic
	The Girl from Alaska	Republic
	Westward Ho	Republic
	The Yukon Patrol	Republic
	Remember Pearl Harbor	Republic
	Romance on the Range	Republic
	The Cyclone Kid	Republic
	Moonlight Masquerade (O: Rose)	Republic
	The Phantom Plainsmen	Republic
	Sons of the Pioneers	Republic
	Hi, Neighbor	Republic
	The Sombrero Kid	Republic
	Joan of Ozark (O: Rose)	Republic
	The Old Homestead	Republic
	Youth on Parade	Republic
1943	*Drums of Fu Manchu*	Republic
1946	*Earl Carroll Sketchbook*	Republic
	(O, A: Arnaud, Butts, Scott)	
1947	*Calendar Girl* (A: Arnaud)	Republic
	Hit Parade of 1947 (A: Arnaud)	Republic

LOUIS FORBES

MUSICAL DIRECTION:

1936	*Mysterious Crossing*	Universal
1937	*She's Dangerous*	Universal
	Let Them Live	Universal
	Night Key	Universal
	Oh, Doctor	Universal
1938	*The Adventures of Tom Sawyer*	Selznick-UA
	Little Orphan Annie	Colonial-Par
1939	*Made for Each Other*	Selznick-UA
	Intermezzo	Selznick-UA
1941	*Pot o' Gold* (A: Adlam, De Vol)	Roosevelt-UA
1945	*Brewster's Millions*	Small-UA
	Getting Gertie's Garter (O: Byrns)	Small-UA
1947	*Intrigue*	Star-UA

1948	*Pitfall*	Regal-UA
1950	*Johnny One-Eye* (O: Strech)	Bogeaus-UA

SCORE:

1949	*The Crooked Way*	Bogeaus-UA
1950	*Second Chance*	Protestant Film Commission
1951	*The Man Who Cheated Himself*	Warner-20th
	Home Town Story	MGM
	A Wonderful Life	Protestant Film Commission

HUGO FRIEDHOFER

1933	*My Lips Betray*	Fox
1938	*The Adventures of Marco Polo*	Goldwyn-UA
	Valley of the Giants (with Deutsch)	WB
1939	*Topper Takes a Trip* (with Powell)	Roach-UA
1943	*China Girl*	20th
	Chetniks	20th
	They Came to Blow Up America	20th
	Paris After Dark	20th
1944	*The Lodger*	20th
	Lifeboat	20th
	Home in Indiana (O: De Packh)	20th
	Roger Touhy, Gangster	20th
	Wing and a Prayer	20th
1945	*The Woman in the Window* (with Lange)	International-RKO
1946	*The Bandit of Sherwood Forest* (O: A. Morton)	Columbia
	So Dark the Night	Columbia
	The Best Years of Our Lives (O: Moross, Cutner, Shuken, Powell)	Goldwyn-RKO
1947	*Wild Harvest* (O: Cutner, Shuken)	Paramount
	Body and Soul	Enterprise-UA
1948	*The Swordsman*	Columbia
	Adventures of Casanova (O: Cadkin)	Eagle Lion
	The Bishop's Wife (O: Moross)	Goldwyn-RKO
	Sealed Verdict	Paramount
	A Song Is Born (MD; O: Burke)	Goldwyn-RKO
	Joan of Arc (O: Moross)	Sierra-RKO
1949	*Enchantment*	Goldwyn-RKO
	Bride of Vengeance (O: Cutner, Shuken)	Paramount
1950	*Three Came Home* (O: Powell)	20th
	Captain Carey, U. S. A. (O: Cutner, Shuken)	Paramount
	No Man of Her Own (O: Cutner, Shuken)	Paramount
	Broken Arrow (O: Powell)	20th

	Edge of Doom (O: Skiles)	Goldwyn-RKO
	Two Flags West (O: De Packh, Hagen)	20th
1951	*The Sound of Fury*	Stillman-UA
	Queen for a Day	Stillman-UA
	Ace in the Hole (O: Cutner, Shuken)	Paramount
1952	*The Marrying Kind*	Columbia
	The Outcasts of Poker Flat	20th
	Lydia Bailey (O: Powell)	20th
	Face to Face	Hartford-RKO
1953	*Thunder in the East*	Paramount
	Above and Beyond	MGM

GEORGE GERSHWIN

1931	*Delicious*	Fox
1937	*Shall We Dance* (O, A: Bennett, Livingston)	RKO
1937	*A Damsel in Distress* (O, A: Bennett, Noble, Bassman)	RKO
1938	*The Goldwyn Follies* (O: Powell;	Goldwyn-UA
	Ballet music: Vernon Duke; MD: Newman)	

IRVING GERTZ

1947	*Dragnet*	Fortune-SG
1948	*Blonde Ice*	Mooney-FC
	The Counterfeiters	Reliance-20th
	Adventures of Gallant Bess	Crestview-EL
	Jungle Goddess	Lippert-SG
1949	*Prejudice*	New World-MPSC
1950	*Destination Murder*	Prominent-RKO
	Experiment Alcatraz	RKO
	Again—Pioneers!	Protestant Film Commission
1951	*Skipalong Rosenbloom*	Kline-UA
	Two Dollar Bettor	Broder-Realart

HERSCHEL BURKE GILBERT

ARRANGEMENTS & ORCHESTRATION:

1946	*Junior Prom* (with Joe Sanns)	Monogram
	Freddie Steps Out (with Sanns)	Monogram
	Secret of the Whistler	Columbia
	The Jolson Story (with Arnaud, Fried, Taylor)	Columbia
1948	*I Surrender Dear*	Columbia

| 1949 | *Manhattan Angel* | Columbia |

SCORE:

1947	*Mr. District Attorney* (O: Sheets)	D.A.-Columbia
1948	*Open Secret**	Marathon-EL
1949	*An Old Fashioned Girl**	Equity-Vinson-EL
	Shamrock Hill	Equity-Vinson-EL
1950	*There's a Girl in My Heart*	Sandre-AA
	(O: Cadkin, Mullendore, Sheets)	
	*The Jackie Robinson Story**	Heineman-EL
	*Three Husbands**	Gloria-UA
1951	*The Scarf**	Gloria-UA
	*The Magic Face**	Briskin-Smith-Col
	*The Highwayman**	Allied Artists
1952	*Without Warning* (O: L. Morton, Mullendore)	Allart-UA
	*Kid Monk Baroni**	Broder-Realart
	Models, Inc.	Chester-Mutual
	*The Ring**	King Bros.-UA
	*The Thief**	Popkin-UA
1953	*No Time for Flowers*	Briskin-RKO

ALBERT GLASSER

1944	*The Monster Maker*	PRC
	The Contender	PRC
1947	*Philo Vance Returns*	PRC
	Gas House Kids in Hollywood	PRC
	Where the North Begins	Bali-SG
1948	*The Return of Wildfire*	Lippert
	Urubu	World Adventure-UA
	Last of the Wild Horses	Lippert
1949	*Valiant Hombre*	Inter-American-UA
	I Shot Jesse James	Lippert
	The Gay Amigo	Inter-American-UA
	Omoo Omoo, the Shark God	Esla-SG
	The Daring Caballero	Inter-American-UA
	Grand Canyon	Lippert
	Satan's Cradle	Inter-American-UA
	Treasure of Monte Cristo	Lippert
	Apache Chief	Lippert
	Tough Assignment	Lippert
1950	*Hollywood Varieties*	Lippert
	The Girl from San Lorenzo	Inter-American-UA

* Orchestration: Joseph Mullendore & Walter Sheets.

	Western Pacific Agent	Lippert
	Everybody's Dancin'	Lippert
	Gunfire	Lippert
	Train to Tombstone	Lippert
	I Shot Billy the Kid	Lippert
	The Return of Jesse James	Lippert
	Border Rangers	Lippert
	Bandit Queen	Lippert
1951	*Three Desperate Men*	Lippert
	Tokyo File 212	RKO
	The Bushwackers	Broder-Realart
1952	*Geisha Girl*	Breakston-Stahl-Realart
	Invasion U.S.A.	American-Columbia

MORT GLICKMAN

SCORE:

1942	*Spy Smasher* (serial)	Republic
	Perils of Nyoka (serial)	Republic
	Shadows on the Sage	Republic
	King of the Mounties (serial)	Republic
	Outlaws of Pine Ridge	Republic
	Valley of Hunted Men	Republic
	The Sundown Kid	Republic
	G-Men vs. the Black Dragon (serial)	Republic
1943	*Thundering Trails*	Republic
	Dead Man's Gulch	Republic
	The Blocked Trail	Republic
	Carson City Cyclone	Republic
	Santa Fe Scouts	Republic
	Calling Wild Bill Elliott	Republic
	Days of Old Cheyenne	Republic
	Riders of the Rio Grande	Republic
	The Man from Thunder River	Republic
	Fugitive from Sonora	Republic
	Bordertown Gun Fighters	Republic
	The Black Hills Express	Republic
	Wagon Tracks West	Republic
	Beyond the Last Frontier	Republic
	Death Valley Manhunt	Republic
	The Man from the Rio Grande	Republic
	Minesweeper	Pine-Thomas-Par
	Overland Mail Robbery	Republic

	Canyon City	Republic
	California Joe	Republic
	Raiders of Sunset Pass	Republic
1944	*Pride of the Plains*	Republic
	The Mojave Firebrand	Republic
	Hidden Valley Outlaws	Republic
	Outlaws of Santa Fe	Republic
	Beneath Western Skies	Republic
	The Laramie Trail	Republic
	Gambler's Choice	Pine-Thomas-Par
1946	*The Mysterious Mr. Valentine*	Republic
1947	*Last Frontier Uprising*	Republic

MUSICAL ARRANGEMENTS:

1944	*Machine Gun Mama*	Schwarz-PRC

MUSICAL DIRECTION:

1943	*Daredevils of the West* (serial)	Republic
1946	*Traffic in Crime*	Republic
	Red River Renegades	Republic
	The Inner Circle	Republic
	Under Nevada Skies	Republic
	Rio Grande Raiders	Republic
	Santa Fe Uprising	Republic
	Stagecoach to Denver	Republic
	The Crimson Ghost (serial)	Republic
1947	*The Magnificent Rogue*	Republic
	Vigilantes of Boomtown	Republic
	Son of Zorro (serial)	Republic
	Homesteaders of Paradise Valley	Republic
	Spoilers of the North	Republic
	Bells of San Angelo	Republic
	Oregon Trail Scouts	Republic
	Web of Danger	Republic
	Jesse James Rides Again (serial)	Republic
	Rustlers of Devil's Canyon	Republic
	The Trespasser	Republic
	Blackmail	Republic
	Marshal of Cripple Creek	Republic
	Along the Oregon Trail	Republic
	The Black Widow (serial)	Republic
	The Wild Frontier	Republic
	Bandits of Dark Canyon	Republic
	Under Colorado Skies	Republic
	G-Men Never Forget (serial)	Republic

1948	*Slippy McGee*	Republic
	Oklahoma Badlands	Republic
	Madonna of the Desert	Republic
	Lightnin' in the Forest	Republic
	California Firebrand	Republic
	The Bold Frontiersman	Republic
	Carson City Raiders	Republic
	Secret Service Investigator	Republic
	The Timber Trail	Republic
	Dangers of the Canadian Mounties (serial)	Republic

ERNEST GOLD

1945	*The Girl of the Limberlost*	Columbia
1946	*Smooth as Silk*	Universal
	The Falcon's Alibi	RKO
	G.I. War Brides	Republic
1947	*Lighthouse*	PRC
	Wyoming (with Scott)	Republic
	Exposed	Republic
1948	*Old Los Angeles*	Republic
1951	*The Family Circus* (cartoon)	UPA-Col
	Georgie and the Dragon (cartoon)	UPA-Col
	Unknown World	Lippert
1952	*Willie the Kid* (cartoon)	UPA-Col
1953	*Gerald McBoing Boing's Symphony* (cartoon)	UPA-Col

MORTON GOULD

1941	*Ring of Steel* (documentary short)	O.W.I.
1945	*Delightfully Dangerous*	Rogers-UA
1946	*San Francisco Conference* (doc. short)	O.W.I.

JOHNNY GREEN

ARRANGEMENTS:

1930	*The Big Pond*	Paramount
	The Sap from Syracuse	Paramount
	Queen High	Paramount
	Animal Crackers	Paramount
	Heads Up	Paramount
	Follow the Leader	Paramount

GREEN *(Continued)*

1931	*Honor Among Lovers*	Paramount
	Night Angel	Paramount

SYNCHRONIZED SCORE AND ARRANGEMENTS:

1931	*Secrets of a Secretary*	Paramount
	My Sin	Paramount
1932	*Wayward*	Paramount
	The Wiser Sex	Paramount

MUSICAL DIRECTION:

1944	*Broadway Rhythm*	MGM
	(O: Duncan, Moore, Oliver, Raymond)	
	Bathing Beauty (O: Duncan, Jackson, Thompson)	MGM
1947	*It Happened in Brooklyn* (O: Duncan)	MGM
1948	*Up in Central Park*	UI
	Easter Parade (O, A: Arnaud, Cutner,	
	Edens, Salinger, Shuken, Van Cleave)	MGM
1950	*Summer Stock*	MGM
	(with S. Chaplin; O: Franklyn, Martin, Salinger)	
1951	*Royal Wedding* (O: Martin, Salinger, Sendrey)	MGM
	An American in Paris	MGM
	(with S. Chaplin; O: Salinger, Sendrey)	
	Too Young to Kiss (underscoring: Cutner, Shuken)	MGM
1952	*Because You're Mine*	MGM

SCORE:

1945	*Weekend at the Waldorf*	MGM
	(underscoring: Cutner; O: Cutner, Duncan, Shuken)	
1946	*The Sailor Takes a Wife* (O: Sendrey, Shuken)	MGM
	Easy to Wed (O: Cutner, Duncan, Sendrey, Shuken)	MGM
1947	*Fiesta* (O: Duncan, Sendrey)	MGM
	Something in the Wind (O: Duncan, Siravo)	UI
1949	*The Inspector General*	WB
1951	*The Great Caruso* (O: Cutner, Sendrey, Shuken)	MGM

MUSICAL SUPERVISION:

1952	*It's a Big Country* (MA: Colombo, Deutsch,	
	Hayton, Kaper, Kopp, Raksin, Rose)	MGM

WALTER GREENE

1945	*Crime, Inc.*	PRC
	Why Girls Leave Home	PRC
1946	*Danny Boy*	PRC
1947	*Wild Country*	PRC

	Range Beyond the Blue	PRC
	Hollywood Barn Dance	Schwarz-SG
	Ghost Town Renegades	PRC
	Black Hills	PRC
	Cheyenne Takes Over	PRC
	Return of the Lash	PRC
	The Fighting Vigilantes	PRC
1948	*Stage to Mesa City*	PRC
	Dead Man's Gold	Western Adventure
	Mark of the Lash	Western Adventure
	Shep Comes Home	Lippert
	Frontier Revenge	Western Adventure
1949	*The Dalton Gang*	Lippert
	Rimfire	Lippert
	Son of Billy the Kid	Western Adventure
	Son of a Badman	Western Adventure
	Square Dance Jubilee	Lippert
	Red Desert	Lippert
1950	*Hostile Country*	Lippert
	Crooked River	Lippert
	Colorado Ranger	Lippert
	West of the Brazos	Lippert
1951	*King of the Bullwhip*	Western Adventure
	Kentucky Jubilee	Lippert
	G.I. Jane	Murray-Lippert
	Yes Sir, Mr. Bones	Spartan-Lippert
	Varieties on Parade	Spartan-Lippert
1952	*Outlaw Women*	Ormond-Lippert
	The Black Lash	Ormond-Realart

FERDE GROFE

ARRANGEMENTS:

1936	*Yankee Doodle Rhapsody* (short)	Paramount

SCORE:

1930	*The King of Jazz*	Universal
1944	*Minstrel Man*	PRC
1950	*Rocketship X M*	Lippert

LOUIS GRUENBERG

1940	*The Fight for Life* (doc.)	U. S. Film Service
1941	*So Ends Our Night*	Loew-Lewin-UA

GRUENBERG *(Continued)*

1942	*Commandos Strike at Dawn*	Cowan-Columbia
1944	*An American Romance* (O: Cutner, *et al*)	MGM
1945	*Counter-Attack*	Columbia
1947	*The Gangster*	King Bros.-AA
1948	*Arch of Triumph* (O: Nussbaum, Raab)	Enterprise-UA
	Smart Woman	Allied Artists
1949	*All the King's Men*	Rossen-Columbia
1950	*Quicksand*	Stiefel-UA

RICHARD HAGEMAN

1938	*If I Were King* (A, AC: Roder; A: Cailliet)	Paramount
1939	*Stagecoach*	Wanger-UA
	(with Harling, Leipold, Shuken; AC: Carbonara)	
	Hotel Imperial (A: Cailliet)	Paramount
	Rulers of the Sea	Paramount
1940	*The Howards of Virginia*	Lloyd-Col
	The Long Voyage Home	Wanger-UA
1941	*This Woman Is Mine*	Lloyd-Univ
1942	*Paris Calling*	Universal
	The Shanghai Gesture	Pressburger-UA
1947	*Angel and the Badman*	Republic
	The Fugitive*	Argosy-RKO
1948	*Fort Apache**	Argosy-RKO
	Mourning Becomes Electra*	RKO
1949	*3 Godfathers**	Argosy-MGM
	She Wore a Yellow Ribbon*	Argosy-RKO
1950	*Wagon Master*	Argosy-RKO

KARL HAJOS

1928	*Loves of an Actress*	Paramount
	Beggars of Life	Paramount
1930	*Morocco*	Paramount
1934	*Four Frightened People*	Paramount
1935	*Manhattan Moon*	Universal
1937	*Two Wise Maids*	Republic
1943	*Hitler's Hangman*	Nebenzal-MGM
1944	*The Sultan's Daughter*	Monogram
	Charlie Chan in the Secret Service	Monogram

---

* Orchestral arrangements by Lucien Cailliet.

	Summer Storm	Angelus-UA
1945	*The Man Who Walked Alone*	PRC
	The Phantom of 42nd Street	PRC
	The Missing Corpse	PRC
	Dangerous Intruder	PRC
	Shadow of Terror	PRC
1946	*The Mask of Diijon*	PRC
	Queen of Burlesque	PRC
	Secrets of a Sorority Girl	PRC
	Down Missouri Way (MD; O: Greene)	PRC
	Driftin' River (MD; O: Greene)	PRC
	Stars Over Texas	PRC
	Wild West	PRC
1948	*Tumbleweed Trail*	PRC
1949	*Search for Danger*	Falcon-FC
	The Lovable Cheat	Skyline-FC
1950	*Kill or Be Killed*	Juno-EL
	It's a Small World	Motion Pictures-EL

LEIGH HARLINE

1938	*Snow White and the Seven Dwarfs* (with Churchill, Smith)	Disney-RKO
1940	*Pinocchio* (with Smith; O: Plumb, Stark, Wolcott)	Disney-RKO
	Blondie on a Budget	Columbia
	Blondie Has Servant Trouble	Columbia
	So You Won't Talk	Columbia
	Blondie Plays Cupid	Columbia
1941	*Mr. Bug Goes to Town*	Fleischer-Par
1942	*The Lady Has Plans* (with Shuken)	Paramount
	The Pride of the Yankees	Goldwyn-RKO
	Careful, Soft Shoulder	20th
	You Were Never Lovelier (MD; O: Cutner; A: Salinger)	Columbia
1943	*They Got Me Covered*	Goldwyn-RKO
	Margin for Error	20th
	The More the Merrier	Columbia
	The Sky's the Limit (O: De Packh)	RKO
	Johnny Come Lately	Cagney-UA
	Government Girl (O: De Packh)	RKO
1944	*Tender Comrade* (O: De Packh)	RKO
	Follow the Boys (MD)	Universal
	A Night of Adventure	RKO

	Heavenly Days (O: De Packh)	RKO
	Music in Manhattan (O: Rose)	RKO
1945	*What a Blonde*	RKO
	Having Wonderful Crime	RKO
	China Sky (O: Bradshaw, Grau)	RKO
	The Brighton Strangler	RKO
	George White's Scandals	RKO
	(Ballets with Lew Brown, Ray Henderson)	
	Johnny Angel	RKO
	Mama Loves Papa	RKO
	First Yank Into Tokyo	RKO
	Isle of the Dead	RKO
	Man Alive	RKO
1946	*Road to Utopia*	Paramount
	From This Day Forward	RKO
	The Truth About Murder	RKO
	Till the End of Time	RKO
	Crack-Up	RKO
	Child of Divorce	RKO
	Lady Luck	RKO
	Nocturne	RKO
1947	*The Farmer's Daughter* (O: Grau)	RKO
	A Likely Story	RKO
	Honeymoon	RKO
	The Bachelor and the Bobby-Soxer	RKO
	Tycoon (O: Grau)	RKO
1948	*The Miracle of the Bells*	RKO
	Mr. Blanding Builds His Dream House	RKO
	The Velvet Touch	RKO
	Every Girl Should Be Married	RKO
1949	*The Boy with Green Hair* (O: Grau)	RKO
	It Happens Every Spring (O: Powell, Spencer)	20th
	The Judge Steps Out	RKO
	The Big Steal	RKO
	They Live by Night	RKO
1950	*The Woman on Pier 13*	RKO
	Perfect Strangers (O: De Packh)	WB
	My Friend Irma Goes West	Paramount
	(O: Cutner, Parrish, Shuken)	
	The Happy Years (O: Plumb)	MGM
1951	*The Company She Keeps*	RKO
	Call Me Mister (O: Hagen, Spencer)	20th
	The Guy Who Came Back (O: De Packh)	20th
	That's My Boy (O: Cutner, Shuken)	Paramount
	His Kind of Woman	RKO

	On the Loose	RKO
	Behave Yourself	RKO
	Double Dynamite	RKO
1952	I Want You	Goldwyn-RKO
	The Las Vegas Story	RKO
	Monkey Business (O: Hagen)	20th
	My Wife's Best Friend	20th
	My Pal Gus (O: Powell)	20th
1953	Taxi	20th

Also many Disney cartoons.

W. FRANKE HARLING

1930	Honey	Paramount
	Monte Carlo (O: Jackson)	Paramount
	The Right to Love	Paramount
1931	Rango	Paramount
1932	Shanghai Express	Paramount
	Broken Lullaby	Paramount
	Fireman, Save My Child	WB
	The Expert	WB
	Play Girl	WB
	One Hour with You (AC)	Paramount
	The Miracle Man	Paramount
	This Is the Night	Paramount
	The Rich Are Always With Us	WB
	Two Seconds	WB
	Street of Women	WB
	Week-End Marriage	WB
	Winner Take All	WB
	Trouble in Paradise	Paramount
	One Way Passage	WB
	Men Are Such Fools	RKO
	Madame Butterfly	Paramount
1933	The Bitter Tea of General Yen	Columbia
	Destination Unknown	Universal
	A Kiss Before the Mirror	Universal
	Cradle Song	Paramount
	A Man's Castle	Columbia
	By Candlelight	Universal
1934	One More River	Universal
	The Scarlet Empress (with Leipold)	Paramount
	The Church Mouse	WB
1935	So Red the Rose	Paramount

1936	*I Married a Doctor*	WB
	The Golden Arrow	WB
	China Clipper	WB
1937	*Mountain Justice*	WB
	Souls at Sea (with Roder; O: Leipold)	Paramount
1938	*Men with Wings* (with Carbonara; A: Cailliet)	Paramount
1939	*Stagecoach*	Wanger-UA
	(with Hageman, Leipold, Shuken; AC: Carbonara)	
1941	*Adam Had Four Sons*	Columbia
	Penny Serenade	Columbia
	Adventure in Washington	Columbia
1942	*The Lady Is Willing*	Columbia
1943	*I Escaped from the Gestapo*	Monogram
	Soldiers of the Soil	Du Pont
1944	*Three Russian Girls*	Rabinovitch-UA
	Johnny Doesn't Live Here Any More	King Bros.-Mon
	When the Lights Go On Again	PRC
1945	*Red Wagon*	American Film Center
1946	*The Bachelor's Daughters*	Stone-UA

ROY HARRIS

| 1940 | *One-Tenth of a Nation* (doc.) | Rockefeller |

MARVIN HATLEY

1936	*Kelly the Second*	Roach-MGM
	Mister Cinderella	Roach-MGM
	General Spanky	Roach-MGM
1937	*Way Out West*	Roach-MGM
	Nobody's Baby (A: Jimmie Grier)	Roach-MGM
	Pick a Star (with A. Morton)	Roach-MGM
	Topper (A: A. Morton)	Roach-MGM
	Our Gang Follies of 1938 (short)	Roach-MGM
1938	*Merrily We Live* (O: A. Morton)	Roach-MGM
	Swiss Miss (O: A. Morton)	Roach-MGM
	Block-Heads	Roach-MGM
	There Goes My Heart	Roach-UA
1939	*Zenobia*	Roach-UA
	Captain Fury	Roach-UA
1940	*A Chump at Oxford*	Roach-UA
	Saps at Sea	Roach-UA

SCORE:

1941	*Married Bachelor* (AC: Kaplan)	MGM
1942	*Dr. Kildare's Victory*	MGM
	Nazi Agent	MGM
	This Time for Keeps	MGM
	Mokey (AC: Kaplan)	MGM
	Maisie Gets Her Man	MGM
	Pierre of the Plains	MGM
	Eyes in the Night	MGM
	Whistling in Dixie	MGM
	Stand By for Action	MGM
1943	*Assignment in Brittany*	MGM
	Pilot No. 5	MGM
	Salute to the Marines	MGM
	Swing Shift Maisie	MGM
1947	*The Hucksters*	MGM
1949	*Any Number Can Play*	MGM
1950	*Battleground*	MGM
	Side Street	MGM
1951	*Inside Straight*	MGM
1952	*Love Is Better Than Ever*	MGM

MUSICAL DIRECTION:

1942	*Born to Sing* (with Snell; O: Heglin, Raab)	MGM
1943	*Best Foot Forward*	MGM
	(O: Arnaud, Bassman, Holmes, Matthias, Salinger)	
1944	*Meet the People*	MGM
	(O: Heglin, Salinger, Watson, Winterhalter)	
1945	*Yolanda and the Thief* (O: Salinger)	MGM
1946	*The Harvey Girls* (O, A: Cutner, Salinger)	MGM
	Ziegfield Follies (MA: Edens; O: Heglin, Salinger)	MGM
1947	*Till the Clouds Roll By* (O: Cutner, Duncan,	
	Franklyn, Heglin, Salinger, Shuken)	MGM
	Living in a Big Way	MGM
	Good News (O: Cutner, Shuken)	MGM
1948	*Summer Holiday* (O: Cutner, Franklyn, Salinger)	MGM
	The Pirate (O: Salinger)	MGM
	Words and Music (O: Salinger)	MGM
1949	*The Barkleys of Broadway* (O: Salinger)	MGM
	On the Town (A: Edens; O: Salinger)	MGM
1951	*Strictly Dishonorable*	MGM
	(original operatic scene: Castelnuovo-Tedesco)	
1952	*Singin' in the Rain* (O: Heglin, Martin, Salinger)	MGM

RAY HEINDORF

ORCHESTRAL ARRANGEMENTS:

1935	*Sweet Music*	**WB**
	Go Into Your Dance	**WB**
1936	*Colleen*	**WB**
	The Singing Kid	**WB**
	Stage Struck	**WB**
	Cain and Mabel	**WB**
	Gold Diggers of 1937	**WB**
1937	*Ready, Willing and Able*	**WB**
	The Singing Marine	**WB**
1938	*Hollywood Hotel*	**WB**
	Gold Diggers in Paris (with Perkins)	**WB**
	Garden of the Moon (with Perkins)	**WB**
	Hard to Get	**WB**
	Going Places (with Perkins)	**WB**
1939	*Naughty but Nice*	**WB**
	On Your Toes	**WB**
	The Roaring Twenties	**WB**
1940	*Brother Rat and a Baby*	**WB**
	It All Came True (with Perkins)	**WB**
	'Til We Meet Again	**WB**
	Knute Rockne—All American	**WB**
1941	*Navy Blues*	**WB**
1942	*Yankee Doodle Dandy* (MA: Roemheld)	**WB**
1943	*This Is the Army*	**WB**
	Thank Your Lucky Stars (with de Packh)	**WB**
1944	*The Desert Song* (MA: Roemheld)	**WB**
	Up in Arms	Goldwyn-RKO
	Hollywood Canteen	**WB**
1945	*Wonder Man* (with Maxwell)	Goldwyn-RKO
	Rhapsody in Blue (AC: Steiner)	**WB**
1946	*Night and Day* (AC: Steiner)	**WB**
	The Time, the Place and the Girl (MA: Hollander)	**WB**
1947	*My Wild Irish Rose* (with Cutter; AC: Steiner)	**WB**
1948	*April Showers*	**WB**
	Romance on the High Seas	**WB**

MUSICAL DIRECTION:

1948	*Two Guys from Texas*	**WB**
1949	*One Sunday Afteroon* (MA: Buttolph)	**WB**
	My Dream Is Yours (O: Cutner, Shuken)	**WB**
	Look for the Silver Lining	**WB**
	(O, A: Cutner, Perkins, Shuken)	
	It's a Great Feeling (O: Cutner, Shuken)	**WB**
	Always Leave Them Laughing	**WB**

1950	*Young Man with a Horn*	WB
	The Daughter of Rosie O'Grady	WB
	(MA: Buttolph; O: De Packh, Perkins)	
	Tea for Two (O: Perkins)	WB
	The Breaking Point	WB
	The West Point Story (O: Perkins)	WB
1951	*Lullaby of Broadway* (O, A: Gilbert, Jackson, Perkins)	WB
	On Moonlight Bay (MA: Steiner)	WB
	Painting the Clouds with Sunshine (O: Perkins)	WB
	Starlift	WB
1952	*I'll See You in My Dreams*	WB
	About Face (O: Perkins)	WB
	She's Working Her Way Through College	WB
1953	*April in Paris* (O: Comstock)	WB
	Stop, You're Killing Me	WB
	The Jazz Singer	WB
	She's Back on Broadway	WB

SCORE:

1951	*Come Fill the Cup*	WB

VICTOR HERBERT

1916	*The Fall of a Nation*	National Films

BERNARD HERRMANN

1941	*Citizen Kane*	Mercury-RKO
	All That Money Can Buy	Dieterle-RKO
1942	*The Magnificent Ambersons*	Mercury-RKO
1944	*Jane Eyre*	20th Century-Fox
1945	*Hangover Square*	20th Century-Fox
1946	*Anna and the King of Siam*	20th Century-Fox
1947	*The Ghost and Mrs. Muir*	20th Century-Fox
1951	*The Day the Earth Stood Still*	20th Century-Fox
1952	*On Dangerous Ground*	RKO Radio
	5 Fingers	20th Century-Fox
	The Snows of Kilimanjaro	20th Century-Fox

WERNER R. HEYMANN

1933	*Adorable*	Fox
1934	*Caravan*	Fox
1937	*The King and the Chorus Girl*	WB

1938	*Bluebeard's Eighth Wife*	Paramount
	(with Hollander; O: Leipold)	
1939	*Ninotchka*	MGM
1940	*The Earl of Chicago*	MGM
	The Shop Around the Corner	MGM
	Primrose Path	RKO
	One Million B. C.	Roach-UA
	He Stayed for Breakfast	Columbia
1941	*This Thing Called Love*	Columbia
	Topper Returns	Roach-UA
	That Uncertain Feeling (O, A: Cutner)	Lesser-UA
	My Life with Caroline	RKO
	Bedtime Story	Columbia
1942	*To Be or Not to Be*	Korda-UA
	The Wife Takes a Flyer	Columbia
	They All Kissed the Bride	Columbia
	Flight Lieutenant	Columbia
	A Night to Remember	Columbia
1943	*Appointment in Berlin*	Columbia
	(AC: Carbonara, Leipold; O: Cutner)	
1944	*Knickerbocker Holiday*	Producers Corp.-UA
	Hail the Conquering Hero	Paramount
	Mademoiselle Fifi	RKO
	Our Hearts Were Young and Gay	Paramount
	My Pal, Wolf	RKO
	Three Is a Family	Lesser-UA
	Together Again (O: Cutner)	Columbia
1945	*It's in the Bag*	Skirball-UA
	Kiss and Tell	Columbia
1947	*Lost Honeymoon*	EL
	Mad Wednesday (O, A: Cutner, Shuken)	Calif.-RKO
1948	*Always Together* (O: Raab)	WB
	The Mating of Millie (O: Gilbert)	Columbia
	Let's Live a Little	United Calif.-EL
1949	*A Kiss for Corliss*	Nasser-UA
	Tell It to the Judge	Columbia
1950	*A Woman of Distinction*	Columbia
	Emergency Wedding	Columbia

FREDERICK HOLLANDER

1934	*I Am Suzanne*	Fox
1935	*Shanghai*	Paramount
1936	*Desire*	Paramount

	Till We Meet Again	Paramount
	Valiant Is the Word for Carrie	Paramount
1937	*John Meade's Woman*	Paramount
	True Confession	Paramount
1938	*Bluebeard's Eighth Wife*	Paramount
	(with Heymann; O: Leipold)	
1939	*Midnight*	Paramount
	Invitation to Happiness (O: Shuken)	Paramount
	Disputed Passage (with Leipold)	Paramount
1940	*Remember the Night*	Paramount
	Too Many Husbands	Columbia
	The Doctor Takes a Wife	Columbia
	Typhoon	Paramount
	(scorer: Krumgold; O, AC: Roder, Shuken)	
	The Biscuit Eater	Paramount
	Safari	Paramount
	The Great McGinty	Paramount
	Rangers of Fortune	Paramount
	South of Suez	WB
1941	*Victory*	Paramount
	Life with Henry	Paramount
	There's Magic in Music	Paramount
	Footsteps in the Dark	WB
	Million Dollar Baby	WB
	Here Comes Mr. Jordan (AC, O: Cutner)	Columbia
	You Belong to Me	Columbia
1942	*The Man Who Came to Dinner*	WB
	Wings for the Eagle	WB
	The Talk of the Town	Columbia
1943	*Background to Danger*	WB
	Princess O'Rourke	WB
1944	*Once Upon a Time*	Columbia
1945	*The Affairs of Susan*	Paramount
	Pillow to Post (O: Moross)	W3
	Conflict (O: Moross)	WB
	Christmas in Connecticut (O: Moross)	WB
1946	*Cinderella Jones* (O: Heindorf, Perkins)	WB
	The Bride Wore Boots (O: Cutner, Shuken)	Paramount
	Janie Gets Married (O: Raab)	WB
	Two Guys from Milwaukee (O: Raab)	WB
	Never Say Goodbye (O: Raab)	WB
	The Verdict (O: Raab)	WB
	The Time, the Place and the Girl (MA; O: Heindorf)	WB
1947	*The Perfect Marriage* (O: Cutner, Shuken)	Paramount
	That Way with Women (O: Raab)	WB

48

	Stallion Road (O: Raab)	WB
	The Red Stallion	EL
1948	*Berlin Express*	RKO
	Wallflower (O: Raab)	WB
	A Foreign Affair (O: Cutner, Shuken)	Paramount
1949	*A Woman's Secret*	RKO
	Caught	MGM
	Adventure in Baltimore	RKO
	Strange Bargain	RKO
	Bride for Sale	RKO
	A Dangerous Profession	RKO
1950	*Born to Be Bad*	RKO
	Walk Softly, Stranger	RKO
	Never a Dull Moment	RKO
1951	*Born Yesterday*	Columbia
	My Forbidden Past	RKO
	Darling, How Could You!	Paramount
1952	*The First Time*	Columbia
1953	*Androcles and the Lion*	Pascal-RKO
	The 5000 Fingers of Dr. T.	Kramer-Col

HOWARD JACKSON

ORCHESTRATION:

1933	*College Humor*	Paramount
	Lady for a Day	Columbia
	Too Much Harmony	Paramount
	I'm No Angel	Paramount
	Sitting Pretty	Paramount
1934	*Palooka*	UA
	Bottoms Up (complete arrangements)	Fox
1948	*Million Dollar Weekend*	Masque-EL

SCORE:

1929	*Hearts in Dixie*	Fox
	Sunny Side Up	Fox
	The Great Gabbo	Sono Art
1933	*Eight Girls in a Boat*	Paramount
	Girl Without a Room	Paramount
1934	*Beloved* (with Victor Schertzinger)	Universal
	Glamour	Universal
1935	*Dizzy Dames*	Liberty
	The Old Homestead	Liberty
	No More Yesterdays	Columbia

49

	The Lone Wolf Returns	Columbia
1936	*Lady of Secrets*	Columbia
	The Music Goes 'Round	Columbia
	Mr. Deeds Goes to Town	Columbia
	Devil's Squadron	Columbia
	And So They Were Married	Columbia
	Counterfeit	Columbia
	The King Steps Out (A: Roder)	Columbia
	Meet Nero Wolfe	Columbia
1939	*The Cowboy Quarterback*	WB
	Pride of the Blue Grass	WB
1940	*An Angel from Texas*	WB
	River's End	WB
1941	*Bad Men of Missouri*	WB
	Three Sons O'Guns	WB
	Law of the Tropics	WB
	The Body Disappears	WB
	You're in the Army Now	WB
1942	*Wild Bill Hickok Rides*	WB
	Bullet Scars	WB
1945	*Club Havana*	PRC
	How Do You Do	PRC
1950	*50 Years Before Your Eyes* (doc.; with Lava)	WB
1952	*This Is Cinerama*	Cinerama Productions

SHORT SUBJECTS:

1939	*Sons of Liberty*	WB
1940	*The Dog in the Orchard*	WB
	Teddy the Rough Rider	WB
1941	*At the Stroke of Twelve*	WB
1943	*Fighting Engineers*	WB
	Mountain Fighters	WB
	Women at War	WB
1949	*March On America!*	WB
	Frontier Days	WB
	All Aboard!	WB
	Pie in the Eye	WB
	Cinderella Horse	WB
	Water Wizards	WB
1950	*Animal Antics*	WB
	Women of Tomorrow	WB
	Just for Fun	WB
	Charlie McCarthy and Mortimer Snerd in Sweden	WB
	Slap Happy	WB
1951	*Anything for Laughs*	WB

	Stranger in the Lighthouse	WB
	Enchanted Islands	WB
	King of the Outdoors	WB
	Winter Wonders	WB
	Hawaiian Sports	WB
1952	*Glamour in Tennis*	WB
	Dutch Treat in Sports	WB
	Stop! Look and Listen	WB
	Switzerland Sportland	WB
	No Pets Allowed	WB
	Land of Everyday Miracles	WB
	California Here I Come	WB
	Centennial Sports	WB
	Cruise of the Zaca	WB

WERNER JANSSEN

1936	*The General Died at Dawn*	Paramount
	(main title & opening sequence: Carbonara)	
1938	*Blockade*	Wanger-UA
1939	*Winter Carnival*	Wanger-UA
	Eternally Yours	Wanger-UA
	Slightly Honorable	Wanger-UA
1940	*The House Across the Bay*	Wanger-UA
	Lights Out in Europe (doc.)	Herbert Kline
1944	*Guest in the House*	Stromberg-UA
1945	*The Southerner*	Loew-Hakim-UA
	Captain Kidd	Bogeaus-UA
1946	*A Night in Casablanca*	Loma Vista-UA
1948	*Ruthless*	Producing Artists-EL
	Safety First (doc. short)	Union Pacific
	Soil (doc. short)	Union Pacific

BRONISLAU KAPER

1940	*I Take This Woman*	MGM
	The Captain Is a Lady	MGM
	We Who Are Young	MGM
	Dulcy	MGM
	Comrade X	MGM
1941	*Blonde Inspiration*	MGM
	I'll Wait for You	MGM
	Rage in Heaven	MGM

	A Woman's Face	MGM
	Barnacle Bill	MGM
	Whistling in the Dark	MGM
	Dr. Kildare's Wedding Day	MGM
	(Symphonic suite by Lionel Barrymore)	
	When Ladies Meet	MGM
	The Chocolate Soldier (MA with Stothart)	MGM
	Two-Faced Woman (O: Arnaud)	MGM
	H. M. Pulham, Esquire	MGM
1942	*Johnny Eager*	MGM
	We Were Dancing	MGM
	Fingers at the Window	MGM
	Crossroads	MGM
	The Affairs of Martha	MGM
	Somewhere I'll Find You	MGM
	A Yank at Eton	MGM
	White Cargo	MGM
1943	*Keeper of the Flame*	MGM
	Slightly Dangerous	MGM
	Bataan	MGM
	Above Suspicion	MGM
1944	*The Cross of Lorraine*	MGM
	The Heavenly Body	MGM
	Gaslight	MGM
	Marriage Is a Private Affair	MGM
	Mrs. Parkington (O: Cutner)	MGM
1945	*Without Love*	MGM
	Bewitched	MGM
	Our Vines Have Tender Grapes	MGM
1946	*The Stranger* (O: Byrns, Cutner)	International-RKO
	Courage of Lassie (with Bradley; O: Sendrey)	MGM
	Three Wise Fools	MGM
	The Secret Heart	MGM
1947	*Cynthia*	MGM
	Song of Love (MD)	MGM
	Green Dolphin Street	MGM
1948	*High Wall*	MGM
	B. F.'s Daughter	MGM
	The Secret Land (documentary)	MGM
1949	*Act of Violence*	MGM
	The Great Sinner	MGM
	The Secret Garden	MGM
	That Forsyte Woman	MGM
1950	*Malaya* (O: Franklyn)	MGM
	Key to the City	MGM

	The Skipper Surpised His Wife (O: Franklyn)	MGM
	A Life of Her Own (O: Franklyn, Heglin)	MGM
	To Please a Lady	MGM
1951	*Grounds for Marriage* (Toy Concertino: D. Raksin)	MGM
	Three Guys Named Mike	MGM
	Mr. Imperium (O: Cutner, Shuken)	MGM
	The Red Badge of Courage	MGM
1952	*Shadow in the Sky*	MGM
	Invitation	MGM
	The Wild North	MGM
1953	*The Naked Spur*	MGM

SOL KAPLAN

SHORTS:

1941	*The Tell-Tale Heart*	MGM
1942	*The Greenie*	MGM
	The Lady and the Tiger	MGM
	Madero of Mexico	MGM
	Unexpected Riches	MGM
1943	*It's a Dog's Life*	MGM
	Self Defense	MGM
	A. T. C. A.	MGM
	Calling All Pa's	MGM
	Victory Vittles	MGM
	Kid in Upper Four	MGM
	Shoe Shine Boy	MGM

FEATURES:

1942	*Tales of Manhattan*	20th Century-Fox
	(O: Bradshaw, Friedhofer, Wheeler)	
1943	*Apache Trail*	MGM
1948	*Hollow Triumph*	EL
1949	*Reign of Terror* (O: Parrish)	EL
	Down Memory Lane	EL
	Trapped	EL
	Port of New York	EL
1950	*711 Ocean Drive*	Columbia
	Mister 880 (O: Powell)	20th
1951	*Halls of Montezuma* (O: Powell)	20th
	I'd Climb the Highest Mountain (O: Powell)	20th
	I Can Get It for You Wholesale	20th
	Rawhide	20th
	House on Telegraph Hill (O: De Packh, Powell)	20th
	The Secret of Convict Lake	20th
	Alice in Wonderland	Lou Bunin

1952	*Red Skies of Montana*	20th
	Return of the Texan	20th
	Kangaroo (O: Powell)	20th
	Diplomatic Courier (O: Powell)	20th
	Way of a Gaucho	20th
	Something for the Birds (O: Mayers)	20th
1953	*Niagara*	20th
	Treasure of the Golden Condor	20th

RUDOLPH G. KOPP

1933	*The Sign of the Cross* (AC, O: Chernis, Roder)	Paramount
1934	*Murder at the Vanities*	Paramount
	(scorer with Wineland; AC, O: Leipold, Jackson, Roder, Lynch, Satterfield, Hand, Reese)	
	Cleopatra	Paramount
	Here Is My Heart	Paramount
	(scorer with Lawrence; C, O: Hand, Satterfield, Leipold, Roemheld, Jackson)	
1935	*All the King's Horses*	Paramount
	(scorer with Lawrence; AC, O: Terr, Roemheld, Leipold, Roder, Hand, Satterfield, Wheeler, Reese, Jackson)	
	The Crusades	Paramount
	(scorers: Lawrence, Krumgold; AC, O: Terr, Hollander, Roemheld, Roder, Hand, Leipold)	
1936	*The Voice of Bugle Ann* (AC: Roder)	MGM
1947	*Gallant Bess* (O: Sendrey)	MGM
	My Brother Talks to Horses (O: Byrns, Franklyn)	MGM
1948	*Tenth Avenue Angel*	MGM
	The Bride Goes Wild	MGM
1949	*The Doctor and the Girl* (O: Cutner, Shuken)	MGM
1950	*Ambush* (AC, O: Sendrey)	MGM
	Mystery Street (O: Cutner, Shuken)	MGM
1951	*Vengeance Valley*	MGM
	Bannerline	MGM
	Calling Bulldog Drummond	MGM
1952	*Fearless Fagan* (MD)	MGM
	The Devil Makes Three (MD)	MGM
1953	*Desperate Search* (MD)	MGM
	The Hoaxsters (MD; doc.)	MGM

ERICH WOLFGANG KORNGOLD

| 1935 | *A Midsummer Night's Dream* | WB |
| | (Arrangement of Mendelssohn) | |

	Captain Blood[1]	WB
1936	*Give Us This Night*	Paramount
	The Green Pastures[1]	WB
	Anthony Adverse[2]	WB
1937	*The Prince and the Pauper*[2]	WB
	Another Dawn[2]	WB
1938	*The Adventures of Robin Hood*[2]	WB
1939	*Juarez*[2]	WB
	The Private Lives of Elizabeth and Essex[2]	WB
1940	*The Sea Hawk*[2]	WB
1941	*The Sea Wolf*[3]	WB
1942	*Kings Row*[1]	WB
1943	*The Constant Nymph*[1]	WB
1944	*Between Two Worlds*[1]	WB
1945	*Devotion*[1]	WB
1946	*Of Human Bondage*[1]	WB
	Deception[4]	WB
1947	*Escape Me Never*[1]	WB

RAOUL KRAUSHAAR

1947	*Stork Bites Man*	Comet-UA
1949	*Arson, Inc.*	Lippert-SG
	Sky Liner	Lippert-SG
	Wild Weed	Franklin
	Zamba	Stearn-EL
	Cowboy and the Prizefighter	Equity-EL
1950	*Prehistoric Women*	Alliance-UA
1951	*The Second Face*	EJLeven-UA
	The Sword of Monte Cristo	Alperson-20th
	Oklahoma Justice	Monogram
	The Basketball Fix	Broder-Realart
	Bride of the Gorilla	Broder-Realart
	Elephant Stampede	Monogram
	The Longhorn	Monogram
	Stage to Blue River	Monogram
1952	*Waco*	Monogram
	The Man from the Black Hills	Monogram
	Rose of Cimarron	Alperson-20th
	(with Edward L. Alperson, Jr.)	

[1] Orchestral arrangements by Hugo Friedhofer.
[2] Orchestral arrangements by Friedhofer & Milan Roder.
[3] Orchestral arrangements by Friedhofer & Ray Heindorf.
[4] Orchestral arrangements by Murray Cutter.

Fargo	Monogram
Untamed Women	Jewel-UA
The Maverick	Allied Artists
Abbott and Costello Meet Captain Kidd	Woodley-WB
1953 *Star of Texas*	Westwood-AA

SIGMUND KRUMGOLD

SCORER:

1934 *Death Takes a Holiday*   Paramount
(with Lawrence; AC, C, O: Leipold, Roder, Kaun, Hand)
We're Not Dressing (with Lawrence)   Paramount
She Loves Me Not   Paramount
(with Wineland; AC, C, O: Satterfield, Mertz)
College Rhythm   Paramount
(with Wineland; C, O: Leipold, Satterfield, Jackson, Mertz, Skiles)

1935 *Mississippi*   Paramount
(with Lawrence; C, O: Leipold, Satterfield, Terr, Hand, Wheeler)
Stolen Harmony   Paramount
(with Setaro; AC, O: Terr, Satterfield, Leipold, Oliver, Goering, Mertz, Grau, Roemheld)
Paris in Spring   Paramount
(with Lawrence; AC, O: Terr, Leipold, Hand, Hollander, Satterfield, Roemheld, Reese)
The Big Broadcast of 1936   Paramount
(with Wineland; AC, O: Terr, Leipold, Satterfield, Bradshaw, Reese)

SCORE:

1939 *Union Pacific*   Paramount
(with Leipold; AC: Carbonara, Shuken)

MUSICAL DIRECTION:

1939 *Honeymoon in Bali*	Paramount
1940 *Golden Gloves*	Paramount
Christmas in July	Paramount
1941 *The Monster and the Girl*	Paramount
One Night in Lisbon	Paramount

GAIL KUBIK

DOCUMENTARIES:

1940 *Men and Ships*   U. S. Maritime Commission

KUBIK *(Continued)*

1942	*The World at War*	O.W.I.
	Paratroops	O.W.I.
	Manpower	O.W.I.
	Dover	O.W.I.
	Colleges at War	O.W.I.
1943	*Earthquakers*	A.A.F.
	The Memphis Belle	A.A.F.
1944	*Air Pattern—Pacifiic*	A.A.F.
1945	*Thunderbolt*	A.A.F.

FEATURES:

1949	*C-Man*	Laurel-FC
1951	*Two Gals and a Guy*	Weisner-UA

CARTOONS:

1950	*The Miner's Daughter*	UPA-Col
	Gerald McBoing Boing	UPA-Col

ARTHUR LANGE

MUSICAL DIRECTION:

1929	*The Mysterious Island* (A: Maxwell)	MGM
	The Hollywood Revue (A: Maxwell)	MGM
1930	*Chasing Rainbows*	MGM
	Flower Garden (short)	MGM
	Pirates (short)	MGM
	Manhattan Serenade (short)	MGM
	The Clock Shop (short; A: Maxwell)	MGM
1931	*The Common Law*	RKO
	A Woman of Experience	RKO
	The Big Gamble	RKO
	Sundown Trail	RKO
	Rebound	RKO
	Devotion	RKO
	Bad Company	RKO
	The Tip-Off	RKO
	Freighters of Destiny	RKO
	Suicide Fleet	RKO
	The Big Shot	RKO
1932	*A Woman Commands*	RKO
	Partners	RKO
	Prestige	RKO
	Panama Flo	RKO
	Lady with a Past	RKO
	Carnival Boat	RKO

	The Saddle Buster	RKO
1933	*Best of Enemies*	Fox
	Life in the Raw	Fox
	Jimmy and Sally	Fox
	Smoky	Fox
1934	*Orient Express*	Fox
	Frontier Marshal	Fox
	Sleepers East	Fox
	Stand Up and Cheer	Fox
	Now I'll Tell	Fox
	The World Moves On	Fox
	Servants' Entrance	Fox
	Marie Galante (MA: Mockridge)	Fox
1935	*Lottery Lover*	Fox
	The County Chairman	Fox
	One More Spring	Fox
	The Little Colonel (MA: Mockridge)	Fox
	It's a Small World	Fox
	Spring Tonic	Fox
	The Daring Young Man	Fox
	Under the Pampus Moon (MA: Mockridge)	Fox
	Doubting Thomas	Fox
	Orchids to You	Fox
	Bad Boy	Fox
	Thanks a Million	Fox
	In Old Kentucky	Fox
1936	*It Had to Happen*	20th Century-Fox
1937	*On the Avenue*	20th Century-Fox
	(A, O: Maxwell, Mockridge, Spencer)	
	Wife, Doctor and Nurse	20th Century-Fox
1938	*Sally, Irene and Mary* (A: Maxwell)	20th Century-Fox
	Rebecca of Sunnybrook Farm	20th Century-Fox
	Hold That Co-ed	20th Century-Fox
1939	*Let Freedom Ring* (O: Raab)	MGM
	The Great Victor Herbert	Paramount

SCORE WITH MAXWELL:

1936	*White Fang*	20th Century-Fox
	Girls' Dormitory	20th Century-Fox
	The Great Ziegfeld (A: Skinner)	MGM
	The Magnificent Brute	Universal
	Under Your Spell	20th Century-Fox
	White Hunter	20th Century-Fox
	Banjo on My Knee	20th Century-Fox
1937	*This Is My Affair*	20th Century-Fox

	Love Under Fire	20th Century-Fox
	Lancer Spy (O: Gerstenberger, Van Loan)	20th Century-Fox
1938	*Kidnapped*	20th Century-Fox
	Three Blind Mice	20th Century-Fox
	We're Going to Be Rich	20th Century-Fox
	Gateway	20th Century-Fox
	Submarine Patrol	20th Century-Fox
1943	*Dixie Dugan*	20th Century-Fox
	Quiet, Please, Murder	20th Century-Fox

SCORE:

1940	*Married and in Love*	RKO
1943	*Lady of Burlesque* (O: De Packh)	Stromberg-UA
	The Dancing Masters	20th Century Fox
1944	*Bermuda Mystery*	20th Century-Fox
	Casanova Brown	International-RKO
	The Woman in the Window (with Friedhofer)	International-RKO
1945	*Belle of the Yukon*	International-RKO
	It's a Pleasure (A, O: Franklyn, Maxwell, Schoepp)	International-RKO
	Along Came Jones	International-RKO
1946	*The Fabulous Suzanne* (O, A: De Saxe)	Republic
1948	*Jungle Patrol*	20th Century-Fox
1950	*The Vicious Years*	Emerald-FC
	The Golden Gloves Story (with Skiles)	Eagle Lion
	Woman on the Run	Fidelity-UI
1951	*The Groom Wore Spurs*	Fidelity-UI
1952	*Japanese War Bride*	Bernhard-20th
	The Pride of St. Louis	20th Century-Fox

ALEXANDER LASZLO

1944	*Black Magic*	Monogram
	Dangerous Passage	Pine-Thomas-Par
	Double Exposure	Pine-Thomas-Par
1945	*High Powered*	Pine-Thomas-Par
	The Great Flamarion	Republic
	One Exciting Night	Pine-Thomas-Par
	Follow That Woman	Pine-Thomas-Par
1946	*Strange Impersonation*	Republic
	The Glass Alibi	Republic
	Hot Cargo	Pine-Thomas-Par
	They Made Me a Killer	Pine-Thomas-Par

	The French Key	Republic
	Joe Palooka, Champ	Monogram
	Accomplice	PRC
1947	*Untamed Fury*	PRC
	Yankee Fakir	Republic
	Banjo	RKO
1948	*The Spiritualist*	EL
	Parole, Inc.	Equity-Orbit-EL
1949	*Tarzan's Magic Fountain*	Lesser-RKO
	Song of India	Columbia
	Amazon Quest	Agay-FC
	Alimony	Equity-Orbit-EL

WILLIAM LAVA

SERIALS:

1938	*Hawk of the Wilderness*	Republic
1939	*Daredevils of the Red Circle*	Republic
	Dick Tracy's G-Men	Republic
	The Lone Ranger Rides Again	Republic
	Zorro's Fighting Legion	Republic

FEATURES:

1938	*Santa Fe Stampede*	Republic
	Red River Range	Republic
1939	*The Night Riders*	Republic
	Three Texas Steers	Republic
	Wyoming Outlaw	Republic
	New Frontier	Republic
	The Kansas Terrors	Republic
	Cowboys from Texas	Republic
1940	*The Courageous Dr. Christian*	RKO
1946	*She-Wolf of London*	Universal
1948	*The Big Punch*	WB
	Embraceable You	WB
	Moonrise	Feldman-Republic
1949	*Flaxy Martin*	WB
	Homicide	WB
	The Younger Brothers	WB
	The House Across the Street	WB
1950	*Barricade*	WB
	Colt .45	WB
	This Side of the Law	WB
	The Great Jewel Robber	WB
	Breakthrough	WB

1951	*Highway 301*	WB
	Inside the Walls of Folsom Prison	WB
	The Tanks Are Coming	WB
1952	*Retreat, Hell!*	WB
	Cattle Town	WB

DOCUMENTARIES:

1945	*To the Shores of Iwo Jima*	UA
	Man on the Land	UPA
	Hydro	U. S. Govt.
1950	*50 Years Before Your Eyes* (with Jackson)	WB

CARTOONS:

| 1951 | *Fuddy Duddy Buddy* | UPA-Col |
| 1952 | *The Dog Snatcher* | UPA-Col |

SHORTS:

1944	*I Won't Play*	WB
1945	*America the Beautiful*	WB
	Hitler Lives	WB
	Good Old Corn	WB
	Star in the Night	WB
	Gem of the Ocean	WB
	Men of Tomorrow	WB
	Sunset in the Pacific	WB
1946	*Smart as a Fox*	WB
	So You Want to Play the Horses	WB
	A Boy and His Dog	WB
	So You Think You're a Nervous Wreck	WB
	So You're Going on a Vacation	WB
	So You're Going to Be a Father	WB
1947	*So You Want to Be a Salesman*	WB
	So You Want to Hold Your Wife	WB
	So You Want an Apartment	WB
	My Own United States	WB
	Power Behind the Nation	WB
	The Man from New Orleans	WB
	Calgary Stampede	WB
	Cavalcade of Egyptian Sports	WB
	Jungle Man Killers	WB
1948	*Sportsmen of the Far East*	WB
	So You Want to Be a Baby Sitter	WB
	So You Want to Be Popular	WB
1949	*Kings of the Rockies*	WB
	Heart of Paris	WB
	Bannister's Bantering Babies	WB

	Drums of India	WB
	Down the Nile	WB
	Let's Go Boating	WB
	Jungle Terror	WB
	Hands Tell the Story	WB
	This Sporting World	WB
	Horse and Buggy Days	WB
	Alpine Champions	WB
	Champions of Tomorrow	WB
	Riviera Days	WB
	Racing Blood	WB
	So You Want to Get Rich Quick	WB
	So You Want to Be an Actor	WB
	Danger Is My Business	WB
	So You Want to Throw a Party	WB
	So You Think You're Not Guilty	WB
	Wish You Were Here	WB
	The Grass Is Always Greener	WB
	My Country 'Tis of Thee	WB
1950	*Grandad of Races*	WB
	So You Want to Move	WB
	So You Want to Hold Your Husband	WB
	Wild Water Champions	WB
	So You Want a Raise	WB
	So You're Going to Have an Operation	WB
	So You Want to Be a Handy Man	WB
	The Will to Win	WB
	The Neighbor Next Door	WB
	The Wanderers' Return	WB
1951	*So You Want to Be a Cowboy*	WB
	So You Want to Be a Paper Hanger	WB
	So You Want to Buy a Used Car	WB
	Every Dog Has His Day	WB
	To Bee or Not to Bee	WB
	Emperor's Horses	WB
	So You Want to Get It Wholesale	WB
	So You Want to Be a Plumber	WB
	So You Want to Be a Bachelor	WB
	Land of the Trembling Earth	WB
	A Laugh a Day	WB
1952	*The Seeing Eye*	WB
	So You Want to Go to a Convention	WB
	So You Want to Enjoy Life	WB
	So You Never Tell a Lie	WB

Note: All scores composed for Warner Bros. orchestrated by Charles
Maxwell.

MAURICE LAWRENCE

1935   *Rhumba*   Paramount
       (scorer with Setaro, Wineland; C, O: Leipold, Satterfield,
       Brito, Hand, Reese, Terr, de Packh)
1937   *The Barrier* (AC: Carbonara)   Paramount

JOHN LEIPOLD

1934	*The Scarlet Empress* (with Harling)	Paramount
1937	*I Met Him in Paris*	Paramount
1939	*Stagecoach*	Wanger-UA
	(with Hageman, Harling, Shuken; AC: Carbonara)	
	Union Pacific	Paramount
	(with Krumgold; AC: Carbonara, Shuken)	
	Disputed Passage (with Hollander)	Paramount
	The Flying Deuces (with Shuken)	RKO
1940	*Geronimo* (with Carbonara)	Paramount
	Santa Fe Marshal	Paramount
	Knights of the Range (with Young)	Paramount
	The Showdown	Paramount
	Stagecoach War	Paramount
	The Quarterback	Paramount
	The Fargo Kid	RKO
1941	*In Old Colorado*	Paramount
	Border Vigilantes	Paramount
	Pirates on Horseback	Paramount
	The Parson of Panamint	Paramount
	Wide Open Town	Paramount
	Riders of the Timberline	Paramount
	Secrets of the Wasteland	Paramount
	Twilight on the Trail	Paramount
1942	*Shut My Big Mouth*	Columbia
	Two Yanks in Trinidad	Columbia
	Blondie for Victory	Columbia
	The Daring Young Man	Columbia
1943	*The Desperadoes*	Columbia
	Good Luck, Mr. Yates	Columbia
	My Kingdom for a Cook	Columbia
	The Heat's On	Columbia
	What a Woman	Columbia
1944	*Nine Girls*	Columbia
1949	*Massacre River* (with Moraweck)	Windsor-AA
	The Big Wheel (with Carbonara, Finston)	Popkin-UA

JOSEPH J. LILLEY

SCORE:

1947	*Variety Girl*	Paramount
	(Puppetoon score: Plumb; O: Van Cleave)	
1949	*The Great Lover* (O: Cutner, Shuken)	Paramount
1950	*Dear Wife* (with Van Cleave)	Paramount
1951	*The Mating Season* (O: Cutner, Shuken)	Paramount

MUSICAL DIRECTION:

1948	*Isn't It Romantic* (MA; O: Van Cleave)	Paramount
1949	*Red, Hot and Blue*	Paramount
	(O: Cutner, Shuken, Van Cleave)	
1950	*Mr. Music* (O: Van Cleave)	Paramount
1951	*At War with the Army*	Paramount
	Here Comes the Groom	Paramount
	(O: Cutner, Shuken, Van Cleave)	
1952	*Sailor Beware*	Paramount
	Jumping Jacks	Paramount
1953	*Road to Bali* (O: Van Cleave)	Paramount
	The Stooge (O: Cutner, Shuken)	Paramount

ALBERT HAY MALOTTE

1932	*A Firehouse Honeymoon* (short)	RKO
1935	*Hi, Gaucho*	RKO
1940	*Dr. Cyclops* (with Carbonara, Toch)	Paramount
1945	*The Enchanted Forest*	PRC

Also many Disney cartoons.

CHARLES MAXWELL

ARRANGEMENTS:

1929	*The Broadway Melody*	MGM
1931	*Trader Horn*	MGM
	Flying High	MGM
1933	*The Prizefighter and the Lady*	MGM

COMPLETE SCORE:

1935	*The Winning Ticket*	MGM
	West Point of the Air	MGM
	Calm Yourself	MGM
1936	*Parole*	Universal
1940	*The Gay Caballero*	20th
1944	*Secrets of Scotland Yard*	Republic
1945	*Scotland Yard Investigator*	Republic
1946	*In Old Sacramento*	Republic

PART SCORE:

1936	*Star for a Night*	20th
1937	*Charlie Chan at the Opera*	20th
1938	*Mysterious Mr. Moto*	20th
1939	*Frontier Marshal*	20th
1941	*Romance of the Rio Grande* (with Mockridge)	20th

SCORE WITH LANGE:

1936	*White Fang*	20th
	Girls' Dormitory	20th
	The Great Ziegfeld (A: Skinner)	MGM
	The Magnificent Brute	Universal
	Under Your Spell	20th
	White Hunter	20th
	Banjo on My Knee	20th
1937	*This Is My Affair*	20th
	Love Under Fire	20th
	Lancer Spy (O: Gerstenberger, Van Loan)	20th
1938	*Kidnapped* (O: Mockridge, Van Loan)	20th
	Three Blind Mice	20th
	We're Going to Be Rich	20th
	Gateway	20th
	Submarine Patrol	20th
1943	*Dixie Dugan*	20th
	Quiet, Please, Murder	20th

DAVID MENDOZA

1925	*The Merry Widow* (O: Baron)	MGM
	The Big Parade (with Axt; O: Baron)	MGM
1926	*Ben-Hur* (with Axt; O: Baron)	MGM
	Don Juan (with Axt; O: Baron)	WB
1928	*White Shadows in the South Seas* (with Axt)	MGM
	Our Dancing Daughters (with Axt)	MGM
1929	*The Trail of '98* (with Axt)	MGM

MAHLON MERRICK

1943	*Silver Skates*	Monogram
	The Girl from Monterey	PRC
1944	*Sensations of 1945* (MD)	Stone-UA
1949	*Alaska Patrol*	Burwood-FC
	Miss Mink of 1949	Wurtzel-20th
	Deputy Marshal	Lippert

MERRICK *(Continued)*

1950	*The Lawless*	Pine-Thomas-Par
	The U.C.L.A. Story	Apex
	The Dupont Story	Apex
1951	*Passage West*	Pine-Thomas-Par
	One Man's Lifetime	Apex
1952	*Red Planet Mars*	Hyde-Veiller-UA

MICHEL MICHELET

1944	*Voice in the Wind*	Ripley-Monter-UA
	The Hairy Ape	Levey-UA
1945	*Music for Millions*	MGM
1946	*Diary of a Chambermaid*	Bogeaus-UA
	The Chase	Nero-UA
1947	*Lured* (O: Gilbert)	Stromberg-UA
1948	*Siren of Atlantis* (O: Gilbert)	Nero-UA
1949	*Impact* (O: Gilbert)	Popkin-UA
	Outpost in Morocco (O: Gilbert)	Moroccan-UA
1950	*The Man on the Eiffel Tower*	A&T-RKO
	Once a Thief	Merit-UA
	Double Deal	RKO
1951	*M*	Columbia
	Tarzan's Peril	Lesser-RKO

CYRIL MOCKRIDGE

Contributed music, adaptation, arrangements, and/or orchestrations to: *David Harum, Handy Andy, Judge Priest, Marie Galante, Captain January, Stowaway, Happy Landing, My Lucky Star,* and *The Little Princess* (all Fox).

MUSICAL DIRECTION:

1935	*The Littlest Rebel*	Fox
1939	*The Hound of the Baskervilles* (PS: Maxwell)	20th
	The Return of the Cisco Kid	20th
	The Adventures of Sherlock Holmes (PS: Raksin)	20th
	Day-Time Wife	20th
	Everything Happens at Night (PS: Maxwell)	20th
1940	*Johnny Apollo*	20th
	Lucky Cisco Kid	20th
	Manhattan Heartbeat	20th
	Pier 13	20th
	The Great Profile	20th

1941	*Golden Hoofs*	20th
	The Cowboy and the Blonde	20th
	A Very Young Lady	20th
	Last of the Duanes	20th
	I Wake Up Screaming	20th
1942	*Young America*	20th
	Rings on Her Fingers	20th
	That Other Woman	20th
1943	*He Hired the Boss*	20th

SCORE:

1942	*Moontide* (with Buttolph)	20th
	Manila Calling (with Buttolph, Raksin)	20th
	The Man in the Trunk	20th
1943	*The Meanest Man in the World*	20th
	Over My Dead Body	20th
	Tonight We Raid Calais	20th
	The Ox-Bow Incident	20th
	Holy Matrimony	20th
	Happy Land	20th
1944	*The Sullivans* (O: De Packh)	20th
	The Eve of St. Mark (O: De Packh)	20th
	Ladies of Washington	20th
	The Big Noise	20th
1945	*Thunderhead—Son of Flika* (O: De Packh)	20th
	Molly and Me (O: De Packh)	20th
	Captain Eddie (O: De Packh)	20th
1946	*Colonel Effingham's Raid*	20th
	Sentimental Journey (O: De Packh)	20th
	The Dark Corner	20th
	Cluny Brown (O: De Packh)	20th
	Claudia and David (O: Powell)	20th
	My Darling Clementine (O: Powell)	20th
	Wake Up and Dream (O: Plumb, A. Morton)	20th
1947	*The Late George Apley* (O: De Packh)	20th
	Miracle on 34th Street (O: Powell)	20th
	Nightmare Alley (O: Hagen)	20th
	Thunder in the Valley (O: De Packh)	20th
1948	*Scudda Hoo! Scudda-Hay!* (O: Hagen, Spencer)	20th
	Green Grass of Wyoming (O: De Packh)	20th
	Deep Waters (O: De Packh)	20th
	The Walls of Jericho	20th
	The Luck of the Irish (O: De Packh, Spencer)	20th
	Road House (O: Hagen, Spencer)	20th
1949	*That Wonderful Urge* (O: De Packh)	20th

	The Beautiful Blonde from Bashful Bend	20th
	Slattery's Hurricane	20th
	Come to the Stable (O: De Packh, Powell)	20th
	I Was a Male War Bride (O: Spencer)	20th
	Father Was a Fullback (O: Virgil)	20th
1950	*Mother Didn't Tell Me* (O: Hagen)	20th
	Cheaper by the Dozen (O: Spencer)	20th
	A Ticket to Tomahawk (O: Hagen, Spencer)	20th
	Love That Brute	20th
	Where the Sidewalk Ends (O: De Packh, Powell)	20th
	Stella (O: Powell)	20th
	American Guerrilla in the Philippines	20th
1951	*You're in the Navy Now* (O: Powell)	20th
	Follow the Sun (O: Powell)	20th
	Half Angel (O: De Packh, Spencer)	20th
	As Young as You Feel (O: De Packh)	20th
	The Frogmen (O: Hagen, Spencer)	20th
	Mr. Belvedere Rings the Bell	20th
	Love Nest (O: Mayers)	20th
	Let's Make It Legal (O: Mayers, Powell)	20th
	Elopement (O: Powell)	20th
1952	*The Model and the Marriage Broker* (O: Mayers, Powell)	20th
	Deadline—U.S.A. (O: Powell)	20th
	Belles on Their Toes (O: Mayers)	20th
	We're Not Married (O: Mayers)	20th
	Dreamboat (O: Mayers)	20th
	Night Without Sleep	20th

LUCIEN MORAWECK

1939	*The Man in the Iron Mask*	Small-UA
1940	*The Lady in Question*	Columbia
	Dreaming Out Loud	Voco-RKO
1941	*International Lady*	Small-UA
1942	*Friendly Enemies*	Small-UA
1946	*Avalanche* (with Garriguenc)	Imperial-PRC
	Strange Voyage	Signal-Monogram
	The Return of Monte Cristo	Small-Col
1947	*High Conquest* (with Garriguenc, Murray)	Monogram
1948	*16 Fathoms Deep* (with Garriguenc)	Lake-Mon
1949	*Massacre River* (with Leipold)	Windsor-AA
1951	*New Mexico* (with Garriguenc)	Allen-UA

JEROME MOROSS

1948	*Close-Up*	Marathon-EL
1951	*When I Grow Up*	Horizon-UA
1952	*The Captive City*	Aspen-UA

ARTHUR MORTON

1935	*Night Life of the Gods*	Universal
	Princess O'Hara	Universal
1937	*Pick a Star* (with Hatley)	Roach-MGM
	Riding on Air	RKO
	Fit for a King	RKO
1939	*The Day the Bookies Wept*	RKO
1940	*Turnabout*	Roach-UA
1947	*Millie's Daughter*	Columbia
1949	*The Walking Hills*	Columbia
1950	*The Nevadan*	Columbia
	Father Is a Bachelor	Columbia
	Rogues of Sherwood Forest (with Roemheld) (O: Gilbert)	Columbia
1951	*Never Trust a Gambler* (O: L. Morton)	Columbia
	The Harlem Globetrotters	Columbia

LYN MURRAY

1947	*High Conquest* (with Garriguenc, Moraweck)	Monogram
1951	*The Prowler*	Horizon-UA
	The Big Night	Waxman-UA
	The Return of Gilbert and Sullivan	Justman-UA
1952	*Son of Paleface*	Paramount
1953	*Pleasure Island*	Paramount
	Here Come the Girls	Paramount

ALFRED NEWMAN

1930	*Campus Sweethearts* (short; MD)	RKO
1931	*Reaching for the Moon*	UA
	Kiki	UA
	Indiscreet	UA
	Street Scene	Goldwyn-UA
	Arrowsmith	Goldwyn-UA
	Tonight or Never	Goldwyn-UA

1932	*Cock of the Air*	Hughes-UA
	Sky Devils	Hughes-UA
	The Greeks Had a Word for Them	Goldwyn-UA
	Mr. Robinson Crusoe	Fairbanks-UA
	The Kid from Spain (MD)	Goldwyn-UA
1933	*Hallelujah, I'm a Bum* (MD)	Milestone-UA
	Secrets	Borzage-UA
	The Bowery	20th Century-UA
	Broadway Thru a Keyhole	20th Century-UA
	Blood Money	20th Century-UA
	Advice to the Lovelorn	20th Century-UA
	Roman Scandals (MD)	Goldwyn-UA
1934	*Gallant Lady*	20th-Century-UA
	Moulin Rouge	20th Century-UA
	Nana	Goldwyn-UA
	Looking for Trouble	20th Century-UA
	The House of Rothschild	20th Century-UA
	Born to Be Bad	20th Century-UA
	Bulldog Drummond Strikes Back	20th Century-UA
	The Cat's Paw	Lloyd-Fox
	The Affairs of Cellini	20th Century-UA
	The Count of Monte Cristo	Small-UA
	The Last Gentleman	20th Century-UA
	Our Daily Bread	Vidor-UA
	Transatlantic Merry-Go-Round (MD)	Small-UA
	We Live Again (O: Powell)	Goldwyn-UA
	The Mighty Barnum	20th Century-UA
	Kid Millions (MD)	Goldwyn-UA
1935	*Clive of India*	20th Century-UA
	Folies Bergere (MD)	20th Century-UA
	The Wedding Night (O: Powell)	Goldwyn-UA
	Les Miserables	20th Century-UA
	Cardinal Richelieu	20th Century-UA
	Call of the Wild	20th Century-UA
	The Dark Angel (O: Powell)	Goldwyn-UA
	Broadway Melody of 1936 (MD)	MGM
	(A: Edens; O: Powell)	
	Barbary Coast (O: Powell)	Goldwyn-UA
	Metropolitan (MD)	20th Century-Fox
	The Melody Lingers On	Small-UA
	Splendor (O: Powell)	Goldwyn-UA
1936	*Strike Me Pink* (MD)	Goldwyn-UA
	These Three (O: Powell)	Goldwyn-UA
	One Rainy Afternoon (MD)	Pickford-Lasky-UA
	Dancing Pirate (MD)	Pioneer-RKO
	Dodsworth (O: Powell)	Goldwyn-UA

	Ramona (O: Friedhofer, Powell)	20th Century-Fox
	The Gay Desperado (MD)	Pickford-Lasky-UA
	Come and Get It (O: Powell)	Goldwyn-UA
	Born to Dance (MD; A: Edens; O: Powell)	MGM
	Beloved Enemy (O: Powell)	Goldwyn-UA
1937	*You Only Live Once*	Wanger-UA
	When You're in Love (MD; O: Powell)	Columbia
	History Is Made at Night	Wanger-UA
	Woman Chases Man (O: Powell)	Goldwyn-UA
	Slave Ship	20th Century-Fox
	Wee Willie Winkie	20th Century-Fox
	(O: Mockridge, Powell)	
	Stella Dallas (O: Powell)	Goldwyn-UA
	Dead End (O: Powell)	Goldwyn-UA
	The Prisoner of Zenda (O: Friedhofer, Powell)	Selznick-UA
	52nd Street (MD)	Wanger-UA
	The Hurricane (O: Powell)	Goldwyn-UA
1938	*Alexander's Ragtime Band*	20th Century-Fox
	(MD; O: Spencer)	
	The Cowboy and the Lady (O: Powell)	Goldwyn-UA
1939	*Trade Winds*	Wanger-UA
	Gunga Din (O: Bennett)	RKO
	Wuthering Heights (O: Powell)	Goldwyn-UA
	Young Mr. Lincoln	20th Century-Fox
	They Shall Have Music (MD)	Goldwyn-UA
	The Star Maker (MD)	Paramount
	Beau Geste (O: Powell)	Paramount
	The Rains Came	20th Century-Fox
	(Hindu music A: Lal Chand Mehra, Buttolph)	
	The Real Glory (O: Powell)	Goldwyn-UA
	Drums Along the Mohawk	20th Century-Fox
	The Hunchback of Notre Dame	RKO
1940	*Little Old New York*	20th Century-Fox
	Broadway Melody of 1940 (MD)	MGM
	(A: Edens; O: Arnaud, Powell)	
	Vigil in the Night	RKO
	The Grapes of Wrath	20th Century-Fox
	The Blue Bird	20th Century-Fox
	Lillian Russell (MD)	20th Century-Fox
	Earthbound	20th Century-Fox
	Maryland (MD)	20th Century-Fox
	Foreign Correspondent	Wanger-UA
	Young People (MD)	20th Century-Fox
	Public Deb No. 1 (MD)	20th Century-Fox
	Brigham Young	20th Century-Fox
	They Knew What They Wanted	RKO

71

	The Mark of Zorro	20th Century-Fox
	Tin Pan Alley (MD)	20th Century-Fox
1941	*Hudson's Bay*	20th Century-Fox
	That Night in Rio (MD)	20th Century-Fox
	The Great American Broadcast (MD)	20th Century-Fox
	Blood and Sand (MD)	20th Century-Fox
	Man Hunt	20th Century-Fox
	Moon Over Miami (MD)	20th Century-Fox
	Charley's Aunt	20th Century-Fox
	Wild Geese Calling	20th Century-Fox
	Belle Starr	20th Century-Fox
	A Yank in the R.A.F. (MD)	20th Century-Fox
	Week-end in Havana (MD)	20th Century-Fox
	How Green Was My Valley	20th Century-Fox
1942	*Remember the Day*	20th Century-Fox
	Ball of Fire	Goldwyn-RKO
	Son of Fury	20th Century-Fox
	Roxie Hart	20th Century-Fox
	Song of the Islands (MD)	20th Century-Fox
	To the Shores of Tripoli	20th Century-Fox
	My Gal Sal (MD)	20th Century-Fox
	Ten Gentlemen from West Point	20th Century-Fox
	This Above All	20th Century-Fox
	The Pied Piper	20th Century-Fox
	Orchestra Wives (MD)	20th Century-Fox
	Girl Trouble	20th Century-Fox
	Springtime in the Rockies (MD)	20th Century-Fox
	The Black Swan	20th Century-Fox
	Life Begins at Eight-Thirty	20th Century-Fox
1943	*The Moon Is Down*	20th Century-Fox
	My Friend Flicka	20th Century-Fox
	Coney Island (MD)	20th Century-Fox
	Heaven Can Wait	20th Century-Fox
	Claudia	20th Century-Fox
	Wintertime	20th Century-Fox
	(MD; PS: Maxwell; Ice Ballet A: Raksin; O: De Packh)	
	Sweet Rosie O'Grady (MD)	20th Century-Fox
	The Gang's All Here (MD)	20th Century-Fox
	(Polka Dot Ballet: Raksin)	
	The Song of Bernadette (O: Powell)	20th Century-Fox
1944	*The Purple Heart*	20th Century-Fox
	Wilson (O: Powell)	20th Century-Fox
	Irish Eyes Are Smiling (MD)	20th Century-Fox
	(O: De Packh, Spencer)	
	Sunday Dinner for a Soldier	20th Century-Fox
	(O: De Packh, Powell)	

1945	*The Keys of the Kingdom* (O: Powell)	20th Century-Fox
	A Tree Grows in Brooklyn (O: Powell)	20th Century-Fox
	A Royal Scandal (O: Powell)	20th Century-Fox
	Diamond Horseshoe (MD)	20th Century-Fox
	(Dream sequence: Raksin; O: Spencer)	
	A Bell for Adano (O: Powell)	20th Century-Fox
	State Fair (MD; O: Powell)	20th Century-Fox
	The Dolly Sisters (MD; O: Rose)	20th Century-Fox
1946	*Leave Her to Heaven* (O: Powell)	20th Century-Fox
	Dragonwyck (O: Powell)	20th Century-Fox
	The Razor's Edge	20th Century-Fox
	Centennial Summer (MD)	20th Century-Fox
	(O: De Packh, Powell, Salinger, Spencer)	
	Three Little Girls in Blue (MD)	20th Century-Fox
	(A, O: Cutner, de Packh, Powell, Shuken)	
	Margie (MD; O: Taylor)	20th Century-Fox
1947	*The Shocking Miss Pilgrim* (MD)	20th Century-Fox
	(Incidental music based on Gershwin songs adapted by Raksin; O: Powell, Spencer)	
	I Wonder Who's Kissing Her Now (MD; O: De Packh)	20th Century-Fox
	Mother Wore Tights (MD; O: Rose)	20th Century-Fox
1948	*Captain from Castile* (O: Powell)	20th Century-Fox
	Call Northside 777 (O: Powell)	20th Century-Fox
	Gentleman's Agreement (O: Powell)	20th Century-Fox
	Sitting Pretty (O: Powell)	20th Century-Fox
	That Lady in Ermine (O: De Packh, Powell, Spencer)	20th Century-Fox
	Cry of the City (O: Hagen, Spencer)	20th Century-Fox
	When My Baby Smiles at Me (MD) (O: Hagen, Spencer)	20th Century-Fox
1949	*The Snake Pit* (O: Powell)	20th Century-Fox
	A Letter to Three Wives (O: Powell)	20th Century-Fox
	Chicken Every Sunday (O: Powell)	20th Century-Fox
	Down to the Sea in Ships (O: Powell)	20th Century-Fox
	Mother Is a Freshman (O: Powell)	20th Century-Fox
	Mr. Belvedere Goes to College (O: Powell)	20th Century-Fox
	You're My Everything (MD) (O: Hagen, Spencer)	20th Century-Fox
	Thieves' Highway (O: Hagen)	20th Century-Fox
	Everybody Does It (MD) (Opera sequence: Castelnuovo-Tedesco)	20th Century-Fox
	Oh, You Beautiful Doll (MD) (O: Powell, Spencer)	20th Century-Fox
	Pinky (O: Powell)	20th Century-Fox

	Prince of Foxes (O: Powell)	20th Century-Fox
1950	*Dancing in the Dark* (MD)	20th Century-Fox
	(O: Hagen, Spencer)	
	Twelve O'Clock High (O: Powell)	20th Century-Fox
	When Willie Comes Marching Home	20th Century-Fox
	(O: Powell)	
	The Big Lift (O: Powell)	20th Century-Fox
	The Gunfighter (O: Powell)	20th Century-Fox
	Panic in the Streets (O: Powell, Spencer)	20th Century-Fox
	My Blue Heaven	20th Century-Fox
	(MD; O: Powell, Spencer)	
	No Way Out (O: Powell)	20th Century-Fox
	All About Eve (O: Powell)	20th Century-Fox
	For Heaven's Sake (O: Powell)	20th Century-Fox
1951	*Fourteen Hours* (O: Powell)	20th Century-Fox
	On the Riviera (O: Hagen, Powell)	20th Century-Fox
	Take Care of My Little Girl (O: Powell)	20th Century-Fox
	David and Bathsheba (O: Powell)	20th Century-Fox
	The Guest (short; O: Powell)	20th Century-Fox
1952	*With a Song in My Heart* (MD)	20th Century-Fox
	(O: Hagen, Spencer)	
	Wait 'Til the Sun Shines, Nellie	20th Century-Fox
	(O: Powell)	
	What Price Glory (O: Powell)	20th Century-Fox
	O. Henry's Full House (O: Powell)	20th Century-Fox
	Stars and Stripes Forever	20th Century-Fox
	(MD; O: Arnaud)	

ALEX NORTH

DOCUMENTARIES:

1937	*Heart of Spain*	Frontier Films
	People of the Cumberland (with Robinson)	Frontier Films
1944	*A Better Tomorrow*	O.W.I.
1945	*Library of Congress*	O.W.I.
	City Pastorale	State Dept.
	Rural Nurse	Willard Pictures

FEATURES:

1951	*The 13th Letter* (O: De Packh)	20th Century-Fox
	A Streetcar Named Desire (O: De Packh)	Warner Bros.
1952	*Death of a Salesman* (O: De Packh)	Kramer-Columbia
	Viva Zapata! (O: De Packh)	20th Century-Fox

	Les Miserables (O: Powell)	20th Century-Fox
	Pony Soldier (O: Powell)	20th Century-Fox
1953	*The Member of the Wedding*	Kramer-Columbia

GEORGE PARRISH

1939	*Exile Express*	Grand National

LOTHAR PERL

1943	*This Land Is Mine*	RKO

EDWARD PLUMB

1942	*Bambi* (with Churchill)	Disney-RKO
	(O: Smith, Steinert, Wolcott)	
1943	*Saludos Amigos* (with Smith)	Disney-RKO
	Victory Through Air Power (with Smith,	Disney-UA
	Wallace; A: Fine, A. Morton, Stark, Vaughn)	
1944	*The Three Caballeros*	Disney-RKO
	(MD with Smith, Wolcott)	
1945	*The Phantom Speaks*	Republic
	Woman Who Came Back	Republic
1951	*Quebec* (with Van Cleave)	Lemay-Templeton-Par

ANDRE PREVIN

1949	*The Sun Comes Up*	MGM
	Scene of the Crime	MGM
	Border Incident	MGM
	Tension	MGM
	Challenge to Lassie	MGM
1950	*The Outriders* (O, PS: Sendrey)	MGM
	Shadow on the Wall	MGM
	Three Little Words	MGM
	(MD; O: Arnaud, Franklyn, Heglin, Salinger)	
	Dial 1119 (O: Heglin)	MGM
1951	*Kim*	MGM
	Cause for Alarm	MGM

LEONID RAAB

| 1948 | *He Walked by Night* | Foy-EL |
| 1949 | *Follow Me Quietly* | RKO |

OSCAR RADIN

1934	*Evelyn Prentice*	MGM
	The Band Plays On	MGM
1935	*Society Doctor*	MGM
	Shadow of Doubt	MGM

DAVID RAKSIN

COMPLETE SCORE:

1937	*The Mighty Treve*	Universal
	She's Dangerous	Universal
	Midnight Court	WB
	Marked Woman	WB
	Let Them Live	Universal
	Wings Over Honolulu	Universal
	Marry the Girl	WB
	San Quentin	WB
1938	*The Kid Comes Back*	WB
1940	*Storm Warning* (doc.)	Paul Burnford
1941	*The Men in Her Life*	Columbia
	Western Daze (Puppetoon)	Pal-Paramount
	Dipsy Gypsy (Puppetoon)	Pal-Paramount
1942	*The Undying Monster*	20th
	Dr. Renault's Secret	20th
1943	*City Without Men*	Columbia
1944	*Inflation* (short)	MGM
	Main Street Today (short)	MGM
	Tampico	20th
	Laura	20th
1945	*Don Juan Quilligan* (O: De Packh)	20th
	Where Do We Go from Here? (O: De Packh)	20th
	Fallen Angel (O: A. Morton)	20th
1946	*Smoky* (O: A. Morton)	20th
1947	*The Homestretch* (O: Powell)	20th
	The Secret Life of Walter Mitty	Goldwyn-RKO
	Forever Amber (O: De Packh, Powell, Spencer)	20th
	Daisy Kenyon (O: Powell)	20th
1948	*Fury at Furnace Creek* (O: De Packh, Spencer)	20th
	Apartment for Peggy	20th
1949	*Force of Evil* (O: L. Morton, R. Raksin)	Roberts-MGM

76

1950	*Whirlpool* (O: Powell)	20th
	The Reformer and the Redhead	MGM
	(O: Arnaud, Franklyn, R. Raksin)	
	Giddyap (cartoon)	UPA-Col
	A Lady Without Passport	MGM
	Right Cross (O: Franklyn, Heglin)	MGM
	The Next Voice You Hear	MGM
	(O: Franklyn, Heglin, R. Raksin)	
1951	*The Magnificent Yankee*	MGM
	Kind Lady	MGM
	The Man with a Cloak	MGM
	Across the Wide Missouri	MGM
	(O: Arnaud, L. Morton, R. Raksin)	
1952	*Sloppy Jalopy* (cartoon)	UPA-Col
	The Girl in White	MGM
	Pat and Mike	MGM
	Carrie (O: Cutner, Shuken, Van Cleave)	Paramount
	Madeline (cartoon)	UPA-Col
1953	*The Bad and the Beautiful*	MGM
	(O: L. Morton, R. Raksin)	

PART SCORE:

1939	*Mr. Moto's Last Warning*	20th
	Frontier Marshal	20th
1941	*Dead Men Tell*	20th
	Ride On, Vaquero	20th
1942	*On the Sunny Side*	20th
	Who Is Hope Schuyler?	20th
	The Man Who Wouldn't Die	20th
	Whispering Ghosts	20th
	The Magnificent Dope	20th
	Through Different Eyes	20th
	The Postman Didn't Ring	20th
	Just Off Broadway	20th
	Manila Calling (with Buttolph, Mockridge)	20th
1945	*Attack in the Pacific* (doc.)	U. S. Navy

KAROL RATHAUS

1939	*Let Us Live*	Columbia
1942	*Jaguas* (doc.)	Viking Fund
1945	*Histadruth* (doc.)	Palestine Labor Union

FREDDIE RICH

1942	*Torpedo Boat*	Pine-Thomas-Par
	I Live on Danger	Pine-Thomas-Par
	Wildcat	Pine-Thomas-Par
	Wrecking Crew	Pine-Thomas-Par
1943	*Stage Door Canteen*	Lesser-UA
	Alaska Highway	Pine-Thomas-Par
	Submarine Alert	Pine-Thomas-Par
	Jack London	Bronston-UA
1944	*A Wave, a Wac and a Marine*	Biltmore-Mon
1945	*A Walk in the Sun*	20th Century-Fox

HUGO RIESENFELD

1915	*Carmen*	Lasky
1920	*Humoresque*	Paramount
1923	*The Covered Wagon*	Paramount
	The Ten Commandments	Paramount
1926	*The Volga Boatman*	Producers Dist. Corp.
	Beau Geste	Paramount
	The Sorrows of Satan	Paramount
	Old Ironsides (with J. B. Zamecnik)	Paramount
1927	*The King of Kings*	Paramount
	Les Miserables	Universal
1928	*Ramona*	UA
	Tempest	UA
	Two Lovers	UA
	The Toilers	T-S
	Sins of the Fathers	Paramount
	The Woman Disputed	T-S
	The Cavalier	T-S
	Revenge	UA
	The Awakening	UA
	Reputation	T-S
1929	*The Rescue*	UA
	Lucky Boy	T-S
	Molly and Me	T-S
	Looping the Loop	Paramount
	My Lady's Past	T-S
	Midstream	T-S
	New Orleans	T-S
	Two Men and a Maid	T-S
	Three Live Ghosts	UA
1930	*Be Yourself*	UA
	One Romantic Night	UA
	The Bad One	UA

	The Lottery Bride	UA
	Hell's Angels	Hughes-UA
1931	*Tabu* (AC: Harling)	Murnau-Par
1933	*Thunder Over Mexico*	Principal
1934	*The Doctor* (short; A: Scharf)	Educational
	Peck's Bad Boy	Principal-Fox
	Little Men	Mascot
1935	*The President Vanishes*	Wanger-Par
	The Wandering Jew	Twickenham
1936	*Let's Sing Again*	Principal-RKO
	Hearts in Bondage	Republic
	Follow Your Heart	Republic
	Daniel Boone	RKO
	The President's Mystery	Republic
	Rainbow on the River	Principal-RKO
	The Devil on Horseback	Condor-GN
	White Legion	Zeidman-GN
1937	*Make a Wish*	Principal-RKO
1938	*Tarzan's Revenge*	Principal-20th
	Wide Open Faces	Loew-Columbia
	Hawaii Calls	Principal-RKO
	Rose of the Rio Grande	Monogram
	The Sunset Murder Case	Grand National

EARL ROBINSON

1937	*People of the Cumberland* (doc.; with North) Frontier Films	
1944	*The House I Live In* (short)	
1947	*The Roosevelt Story* (doc.)	Tola-UA
	The Man from Texas (O: Cadkin)	Eagle Lion
1948	*Muscle Beach* (doc. short)	

MILAN RODER
PART SCORE:

1932	*Silver Dollar*	WB
1935	*The Lives of a Bengal Lancer*	Paramount
	The Last Outpost	Paramount
	Last of the Pagans	MGM
1936	*Too Many Parents*	Paramount
1937	*Easy Living*	Paramount
	Exclusive	Paramount
	Souls at Sea (with Harling; O: Leipold)	Paramount
1938	*Bulldog Drummond in Africa*	Paramount
1939	*Never Say Die*	Paramount

1933	*Golden Harvest*	Paramount
1934	*Imitation of Life*	Universal
	The Man Who Reclaimed His Head	Universal
1935	*Kliou (The Tiger)*	Bennett-RKO
	Mary Burns, Fugitive	Wanger-Par
1936	*Dracula's Daughter*	Universal
	Three Smart Girls	Universal
1937	*Stand-In*	Wanger-UA
1938	*I Met My Love Again*	Wanger-UA
	Four's a Crowd	WB
	Comet Over Broadway	WB
1939	*Nancy Drew, Reporter*	WB
	You Can't Get Away with Murder	WB
	Invisible Stripes	WB
1940	*A Child Is Born*	WB
	Brother Rat and a Baby	WB
	British Intelligence	WB
	*Brother Orchid**	WB
	*The Man Who Talked Too Much**	WB
	*My Love Came Back**	WB
	*No Time for Comedy**	WB
	Lady with Red Hair	WB
1941	*Four Mothers**	WB
	*Honeymoon for Three**	WB
	*Flight from Destiny**	WB
	*The Strawberry Blonde**	WB
	*The Wagons Roll at Night**	WB
	*Affectionately Yours**	WB
	*Blues in the Night**	WB
1942	*Always in My Heart* (O: Perkins)	WB
	*The Male Animal**	WB
	*Gentleman Jim**	WB
	Yankee Doodle Dandy (MA)*	WB
1943	*The Hard Way**	WB
1944	*The Desert Song* (MA)*	WB
	Shine On, Harvest Moon (MA; O: Perkins)	WB
	Make Your Own Bed	WB
	Janie	WB
1945	*Too Young to Know*	WB
1946	*O.S.S.* (with Amfitheatrof; O: Cutner, Shuken)	Paramount
	Mr. Ace	Bogeaus-UA
1947	*Curley*	Roach-UA
	The Fabulous Joe	Roach-UA
	Heaven Only Knows	Nero-UA

---

* Orchestral arrangements by Ray Heindorf.

80

ROEMHELD *(Continued)*

Down to Earth (with Duning; Greek ballet
    music: Castelnuovo-Tedesco; O: Hagen, Gilbert) Columbia
Christmas Eve (O: Gilbert)   Bogeaus-UA
The Flame   Republic
It Had to Be You (O: Gilbert)   Columbia

1948 *Here Comes Trouble*   Roach-UA
      Who Killed Doc Robbin?   Roach-UA
      The Lady from Shanghai (O: Gilbert)   Columbia
      I, Jane Doe   Republic
      On Our Merry Way (A: Russell, Gilbert)   Bogeaus-UA
      The Fuller Brush Man (O: Gilbert)   Columbia
      The Girl from Manhattan (A: Heglin)   Bogeaus-UA
      Station West   RKO
      My Dear Secretary (O: Gilbert)   Popkin-UA

1949 *The Lucky Stiff*   Amusement Enterprises-UA
      Mr. Soft Touch (O: Gilbert)   Columbia
      Miss Grant Takes Richmond   Columbia

1950 *Kill the Umpire*   Columbia
      (O: Gilbert, A. Morton, Mullendore)
      The Good Humor Man (O: Gilbert)   Columbia
      Rogues of Sherwood Forest (with Morton)   Columbia
      (O: Gilbert)
      The Fuller Brush Girl (O: Gilbert)   Columbia

1951 *Valentino*   Columbia

1952 *Chicago Calling*   Arrowhead-UA
      The Big Trees (O: Cutner, de Packh, Shuken)   WB
      Jack and the Beanstalk   Exclusive-WB
      3 for Bedroom C   Brenco-WB

1953 *Ruby Gentry*   Bernhard-Vidor-20th

SIGMUND ROMBERG

1922 *Foolish Wives*   Universal

DAVID ROSE

1944 *Resisting Enemy Interrogation* (doc.)   A.A.F.
      The Princess and the Pirate   Goldwyn-RKO
      Winged Victory (O: De Packh)   20th

1950 *The Underworld Story* (O: Cadkin)   Chester-UA

1951 *Rich, Young and Pretty* (MD)   MGM
      Texas Carnival (MD; O: Sendrey)   MGM

1952 *Just This Once*   MGM

	Young Man with Ideas	**MGM**
	Everything I Have Is Yours (MD)	MGM
1953	*The Clown*	MGM
	Confidentially Connie	MGM

MILTON ROSEN

1943	*He's My Guy*	Universal
1944	*Enter Arsene Lupin*	Universal
1945	*Sudan*	Universal
	Swing Out, Sister	Universal
	On Stage Everybody	Universal
	Shady Lady	Universal
	Men in Her Diary	Universal
1946	*Tangier*	Universal
	The Spider Woman Strikes Back	Universal
	Dressed to Kill (MD)	Universal
	Cuban Pete	Universal
	Slightly Scandalous	Universal
	Rustler's Round-up (MD)	Universal
	The Time of Their Lives	Universal
	Lawless Breed (MD)	Universal
	White Tie and Tails	Universal
1947	*Slave Girl* (O: Tamkin)	UI
	Pirates of Monterey	UI
1948	*Abraham and Isaac*	Churchcraft
	Daniel in the Lions Den	Churchcraft
	Of Such Is the Kingdom	Churchcraft
	The Raising of Lazarus	Churchcraft
	Bob and Sally	Social Guidance
	The Challenge	Reliance-20th
	13 Lead Soldiers	Reliance-20th
	The Creeper	Reliance-20th
1950	*The Milkman*	UI

MIKLOS ROZSA

1937	*Knight Without Armor*	Korda-UA
	Thunder in the City	Atlantic-Columbia
	Murder on Diamond Row	Korda-UA
	(British title: *The Squeaker*)	
	The Green Cockatoo	Korda-UA
	(British title: *Four Dark Hours*)	
1938	*The Divorce of Lady X*	Korda-UA
1939	*The Four Feathers*	Korda-UA

82

	U-Boat 29	Asher-Columbia
	(British title: *The Spy in Black*)	
	Missing Ten Days	Asher-Columbia
	(British title: *Ten Days in Paris*)	
1940	*The Fugitive*	Somlo-Universal
	(British title: *On the Night of the Fire*)	
	The Thief of Bagdad	Korda-UA
1941	*That Hamilton Woman*	Korda-UA
	(British title: *Lady Hamilton*)	
	Lydia	Korda-UA
	Sundown	Wanger-UA
1942	*Jungle Book*	Korda-UA
	Jacare (documentary)	Mayfair-UA
1943	*Five Graves to Cairo*	Paramount
	So Proudly We Hail	Paramount
	Sahara (O: Cutner)	Columbia
	The Woman of the Town	Sherman-UA
1944	*The Hour Before the Dawn*	Paramount
	Double Indemnity	Paramount
	The Man in Half Moon Street	Paramount
	Dark Waters	Bogeaus-UA
1945	*Blood on the Sun*	Cagney-UA
	Lady on a Train	Universal
	The Lost Weekend (O: Cutner, Shuken)	Paramount
	Spellbound	Selznick-UA
1946	*Because of Him*	Universal
	The Killers	Universal
	The Strange Love of Martha Ivers	Paramount
1947	*The Red House*	Thalia-UA
	The Macomber Affair	Bogeaus-UA
	Time Out of Mind	UI
	(with Castelnuovo-Tedesco; O: Cutner, Shuken)	
	The Other Love	Enterprise-UA
	Brute Force	UI
	Desert Fury	Paramount
1948	*A Woman's Vengeance*	UI
	Secret Beyond the Door	UI
	A Double Life	UI
	The Naked City (with Skinner)	UI
	Kiss the Blood Off My Hands	UI
1949	*Criss Cross*	UI
	Command Decision	MGM
	The Bribe	MGM
	Madame Bovary	MGM
	The Red Danube	MGM
	Adam's Rib	MGM

1950	East Side, West Side	MGM
	The Asphalt Jungle	MGM
	Crisis	MGM
1951	Quo Vadis	MGM
	The Light Touch (AC: Wolcott)	MGM
1952	Ivanhoe	MGM
	Plymouth Adventure (O: Franklyn)	MGM
1953	The Story of Three Loves	MGM
	Julius Caesar	MGM

MUSICAL ADAPTATION:

1941	New Wine (Schubert)	Gloria-UA
1945	A Song to Remember (Chopin)	Columbia
1947	Song of Scheherazade (Rimsky-Korsakov)	UI
1950	The Miniver Story (Stothart)	MGM

Note: Before 1941, Rozsa orchestrated his own music. From *That Hamilton Woman* to date his scores have been orchestrated by Eugene Zador.

HENRY RUSSELL

| 1948 | Lulu Belle | Bogeaus-Columbia |
| 1951 | Five (O: Maxwell) | Lobo-Columbia |

CONRAD SALINGER

1951	The Unknown Man	MGM
1952	Carbine Williams	MGM
	Washington Story	MGM
	The Prisoner of Zenda (MA of Newman's 1937 score)	MGM

HANS J. SALTER

MUSICAL DIRECTION:

1939	Call a Messenger	Universal
	The Big Guy	Universal
1940	Framed	Universal
	Zanzibar	Universal
	Black Friday	Universal
	Enemy Agent	Universal
	Ski Patrol	Universal
	Alias the Deacon	Universal
	Love, Honor and Oh, Baby!	Universal
	I Can't Give You Anything But Love, Baby	Universal

Private Affairs	Universal
Black Diamonds	Universal
You're Not So Tough	Universal
South to Karanga	Universal
The Leatherpushers	Universal
The Mummy's Hand	Universal
Diamond Frontier	Universal
Slightly Tempted	Universal
Law and Order	Universal
I'm Nobody's Sweetheart Now	Universal
The Devil's Pipeline	Universal
Sandy Gets Her Man	Universal
Meet the Wildcat	Universal
Margie	Universal
Trail of the Vigilantes	Universal
Give Us Wings	Universal
1941 *Where Did You Get That Girl?*	Universal
Lucky Devils	Universal
San Francisco Docks	Universal
Meet the Chump	Universal
Dark Streets of Cairo	Universal
Mr. Dynamite	Universal
Double Date	Universal
The Man Who Lost Himself	Universal
Horror Island	Universal
Man Made Monster	Universal
Model Wife	Universal
Mutiny in the Arctic	Universal
The Black Cat	Universal
Men of the Timberland	Universal
Tight Shoes	Universal
Hit the Road	Universal
Bachelor Daddy	Universal
Hello Sucker	Universal
Raiders of the Desert	Universal
Hold That Ghost	Universal
A Dangerous Game	Universal
Badlands of Dakota	Universal
Mob Town	Universal
Burma Convoy	Universal
Flying Cadets	Universal
Arizona Cyclone	Universal
Sealed Lips	Universal
Road Agent	Universal
1942 *North to the Klondike*	Universal
Treat 'Em Rough	Universal

	Bombay Clipper	Universal
	Stagecoach Buckaroo	Universal
	The Mad Doctor of Market Street	Universal
	Frisco Lil	Universal
	The Mystery of Marie Roget	Universal
	The Strange Case of Doctor Rx	Universal
	Fighting Bill Fargo	Universal
	You're Telling Me	Universal
	Tough as They Come	Universal
	The Silver Bullet	Universal
	Top Sergeant	Universal
	There's One Born Every Minute	Universal
	Danger in the Pacific	Universal
	Drums of the Congo	Universal
	Invisible Agent	Universal
	Timber	Universal
	Boss of Hangtown Mesa	Universal
	Half Way to Shanghai	Universal
	Deep in the Heart of Texas	Universal
	Sin Town	Universal
	Destination Unknown	Universal
	The Mummy's Tomb	Universal
	Night Monster	Universal
	Little Joe, the Wrangler	Universal
	Madame Spy	Universal
	The Old Chisholm Trail	Universal
	The Great Impersonation	Universal
1943	*Eyes of the Underworld*	Universal
	Mug Town	Universal
	Tenting Tonight on the Old Camp Ground	Universal
	Hi'Ya Chum	Universal
	Frankenstein Meets the Wolf Man	Universal
	Keep 'Em Slugging	Universal
	Cheyenne Roundup	Universal
	Cowboy in Manhattan	Universal
	Captive Wild Woman	Universal
	Raiders of San Joaquin	Universal
	Get Going	Universal
	Frontier Badmen	Universal
	The Lone Star Trail	Universal
	Sherlock Holmes Faces Death	Universal
	Arizona Trail	Universal
	Hi'Ya Sailor	Universal
	The Mad Ghoul	Universal
	Never a Dull Moment	Universal
1944	*Marshal of Gunsmoke*	Universal

	Sherlock Holmes and the Spider Woman	Universal
	Phantom Lady	Universal
	Hat Check Honey	Universal
	Hi, Good Lookin'	Universal
	Pardon My Rhythm	Universal
	Boss of Boomtown	Universal
	The Mummy's Ghost	Universal
	Twilight on the Prairie	Universal
	Allergic to Love	Universal
	The Merry Monahans	Universal
1945	*See My Lawyer*	Universal
	I'll Tell the World	Universal
	The Frozen Ghost	Universal
	Easy to Look At	Universal
	The Strange Affair of Uncle Harry	Universal
	River Gang	Universal
1946	*House of Horrors*	Universal
	Her Adventurous Night	Universal
	The Dark Horse	Universal
	Little Miss Big	Universal

SCORE:

1940	*The Invisible Man Returns* (with Skinner)	Universal
	Seven Sinners (with Skinner)	Universal
1941	*It Started with Eve*	Universal
1942	*The Ghost of Frankenstein*	Universal
	The Spoilers	Universal
	Pittsburgh (with Skinner)	Universal
1943	*The Amazing Mrs. Holliday* (with Skinner)	Universal
	The Strange Death of Adolph Hitler	Universal
	Son of Dracula	Universal
	His Butler's Sister	Universal
1944	*The Invisible Man's Revenge*	Universal
	Christmas Holiday	Universal
	San Diego, I Love You	Universal
	Can't Help Singing (O: Skinner)	Universal
1945	*House of Frankenstein*	Universal
	Patrick the Great	Universal
	That's the Spirit	Universal
	That Night with You (MA)	Universal
	This Love of Ours	Universal
	Scarlet Street	Universal
1946	*So Goes My Love*	Universal
	Lover Come Back	Universal
	Magnificent Doll (O: Tamkin)	Universal
1947	*Michigan Kid*	Universal

	That's My Man	Republic
	The Web (O: Tamkin)	UI
	Love from a Stranger (O: Cadkin)	EL
1948	*The Sign of the Ram* (O: Gilbert)	Signet-Columbia
	Man-Eater of Kumaon	UI
	An Innocent Affair	Nasser-UA
1949	*Cover-Up* (O: Byrns)	Nasser-UA
	The Reckless Moment	Wanger-Columbia
1950	*Borderline*	UI
	Please Believe Me (O: Byrns)	MGM
	The Killer That Stalked New York (O: Byrns, A. Morton)	Columbia
1951	*Frenchie*	UI
	Tomahawk	UI
	Apache Drums	UI
	The Prince Who Was a Thief	UI
	Thunder on the Hill	UI
	You Never Can Tell	UI
	The Golden Horde	UI
1952	*Finders Keepers*	UI
	Bend of the River	UI
	Flesh and Fury	UI
	The Battle at Apache Pass	UI
	Untamed Frontier	UI
	Against All Flags	UI

PAUL SAWTELL

1940	*Legion of the Lawless*	RKO
	Mexican Spitfire	RKO
	Little Orvie	RKO
	Millionaire Playboy	RKO
	Bullet Code	RKO
	Prairie Law	RKO
	Pop Always Pays	RKO
	Stage to Chino	RKO
	Wagon Train	RKO
1941	*Along the Rio Grande*	RKO
	Robbers of the Range	RKO
	Redhead	Monogram
	Six Gun Gold	RKO
	The Bandit Trail	RKO
	The Gay Falcon	RKO
	No Hands on the Clock	Paramount
1942	*A Date with the Falcon*	RKO

	Valley of the Sun	RKO
	Land of the Open Range	RKO
	Scattergood Rides High	RKO
	Come On, Danger	RKO
	Thundering Hoofs	RKO
	Hillbilly Blitzkrieg	Monogram
	Scattergood Survives a Murder	RKO
	Red River Robin Hood	RKO
	Bandit Ranger	RKO
	Pirates of the Prairie	RKO
1943	*The Great Gildersleeve*	RKO
	Fighting Frontier	RKO
	Cinderella Swings It	RKO
	Tarzan Triumphs	RKO
	Sagebrush Law	RKO
	The Avenging Rider	RKO
	Tarzan's Desert Mystery	RKO
	Calling Dr. Death	Universal
1944	*Oklahoma Raiders*	Universal
	Weird Woman	Universal
	The Scarlet Claw	Universal
	Youth Runs Wild	RKO
	Gildersleeve's Ghost	RKO
	Secret Command	Columbia
	Mr. Winkle Goes to War (with Dragon)	Columbia
	Trail to Gunsight	Universal
	The Pearl of Death	Universal
	Dead Man's Eyes	Universal
	Riders of the Santa Fe	Universal
	The Old Texas Trail	Universal
1945	*Nevada*	RKO
	The Mummy's Curse	Universal
	The House of Fear	Universal
	The Power of the Whistler	Columbia
	The Fighting Guardsman	Columbia
	Tarzan and the Amazons	RKO
	Renegades of the Rio Grande	Universal
	Jungle Captive	Universal
	West of the Pecos	RKO
	The Falcon in San Francisco	RKO
	Wanderer of the Wasteland	RKO
	I Love a Bandleader	Columbia
	The Crime Doctor's Warning	Columbia
	Snafu	Columbia
1946	*A Game of Death*	RKO
	Tarzan and the Leopard Woman	RKO

	Perilous Holiday	Columbia
	Strange Conquest	Universal
	The Cat Creeps	Universal
	Renegades	Columbia
	Danger Woman	Universal
	Wild Beauty	Universal
	Step by Step	RKO
	Sunset Pass	RKO
	Criminal Court	RKO
	Vacation in Reno	RKO
	The Falcon's Adventure	RKO
	San Quentin	RKO
	Alias Mr. Twilight	Columbia
1947	*Blind Spot*	Columbia
	Trail Street	RKO
	The Devil Thumbs a Ride	RKO
	Code of the West	RKO
	Tarzan and the Huntress	RKO
	Born to Kill	RKO
	Thunder Mountain	RKO
	Desperate	RKO
	Dick Tracy's Dilemma	RKO
	The Vigilantes Return	UI
	Keeper of the Bees	Columbia
	Under the Tonto Rim	RKO
	Seven Keys to Baldpate	RKO
	Dick Tracy Meets Gruesome	RKO
	Wild Horse Mesa	RKO
1948	*For You I Die*	Arpi-FC
	T-Men (O: Cadkin)	Small-EL
	Western Heritage	RKO
	The Arizona Ranger	RKO
	Raw Deal	Small-EL
	River Lady (O: Tamkin)	UI
	Guns of Hate	RKO
	Mystery in Mexico	RKO
	Four Faces West	Enterprise-UA
	Return of the Badmen	RKO
	Design for Death (doc.)	RKO
	The Black Arrow	Small-Col
	Bodyguard	RKO
	Northwest Stampede (O: Cadkin)	EL
	Walk a Crooked Mile	Small-Col
	Gun Smugglers	RKO
1949	*Brothers in the Saddle*	RKO
	Bad Boy	AA

	The Clay Pidgeon	RKO
	The Big Cat	Moss-EL
	Rustlers	RKO
	Stagecoach Kid	RKO
	The Doolins of Oklahoma (with Duning)	Columbia
	The Mysterious Desperado	RKO
	Savage Splendor (doc.)	RKO
	Masked Raiders	RKO
	The Threat	RKO
	Fighting Man of the Plains	Holt-20th
1950	*Davy Crockett, Indian Scout*	Small-UA
	Riders of the Range	RKO
	Tarzan and the Slave Girl	RKO
	Storm Over Wyoming	RKO
	Fortunes of Captain Blood	Columbia
	(O: Cadkin, Gilbert, Raab)	
	Rider from Tucson	RKO
	Dynamite Pass	RKO
	The Cariboo Trail	Holt-20th
	Border Treasure	RKO
	Bunco Squad	RKO
	Outrage	RKO
	Rio Grande Patrol	RKO
	Southside 1-1000	AA
	Rogue River	Ventura-EL
	Hunt the Man Down	RKO
1951	*Stage to Tucson* (O: Gilbert)	Columbia
	The Great Missouri Raid	Holt-Par
	Law of the Badlands	RKO
	Santa Fe (O: Gilbert)	Columbia
	Saddle Legion	RKO
	Gun Play	RKO
	Jungle Headhunters (doc.)	RKO
	Best of the Badmen	RKO
	Roadblock	RKO
	Pistol Harvest	RKO
	Warpath	Holt-Par
	Hot Lead	RKO
	The Whip Hand	RKO
	The Son of Dr. Jekyll	Columbia
	Fort Defiance	Ventura-UA
	Silver City	Holt-Par
	Overland Telegraph	RKO
1952	*Flaming Feather*	Holt-Par
	Trail Guide	RKO
	Road Agent	RKO

	Tarzan's Savage Fury	RKO
	Target	RKO
	The Half-Breed	RKO
	Denver & Rio Grande	Holt-Par
	Hurricane Smith	Holt-Par
	The Savage	Paramount
	Sky Full of Moon	MGM
1953	*Kansas City Confidential*	Small-UA

WALTER SCHARF

MUSICAL DIRECTION:

1942	*Secrets of the Underground*	Republic
	Ice Capades Revue	Republic
	Johnny Doughboy (O: Rose)	Republic
1943	*London Blackout Murders*	Republic
	Hit Parade of 1943 (O: Skiles)	Republic
	Shantytown	Republic
	Chatterbox	Republic
	Thumbs Up	Republic
	Someone to Remember	Republic
	Nobody's Darling (O: Skiles)	Republic
	Sleepy Lagoon	Republic
1944	*Hands Across the Border* (O: Skiles)	Republic
	Casanova in Burlesque	Republic
	Cowboy and the Senorita (PS: Maxwell)	Republic
	Atlantic City (O: Dubin)	Republic
	Brazil (O: Parrish)	Republic
	Lake Placid Serenade (PS: Maxwell)	Republic
1945	*Earl Carroll Vanities* (A: Dubin; O: Parrish)	Republic
	Mexicana (O: Dubin)	Republic
1946	*Murder in the Music Hall*	Republic
	(Ice ballet: Dubin; O: de Saxe; PS, O: Plumb; A: Butts)	
	I've Always Loved You	Republic
1952	*Hans Christian Andersen* (O: Moross)	Goldwyn-RKO

ARRANGEMENTS:

1948	*Casbah*	UI
	Are You With It?	UI
	Mexican Hayride	UI

SCORE:

1943	*In Old Oklahoma*	Republic
1944	*The Fighting Seabees*	Republic
	The Lady and the Monster (O: Skiles)	Republic

	Storm Over Lisbon	Republic
1945	*The Cheaters*	Republic
	Dakota	Republic
1948	*The Saxon Charm* (O: Tamkin)	UI
	The Countess of Monte Cristo (O: Tamkin)	UI
1949	*Red Canyon*	UI
	City Across the River	UI
	Take One False Step	UI
	Yes Sir, That's My Baby	UI
	Abandoned	UI
1950	*South Sea Sinner*	UI
	Buccaneer's Girl	UI
	Curtain Call at Cactus Creek	UI
	Sierra	UI
	Spy Hunt	UI
	Deported (O: Tamkin)	UI
1951	*Two Tickets to Broadway* (O: Cutner, Shuken)	RKO

RUDOLPH SCHRAGER

1942	*Snuffy Smith, Yard Bird*	Monogram
1944	*Career Girl*	PRC
	Dixie Jamboree	PRC
	Take It Big	Pine-Thomas-Par
1946	*People Are Funny*	Pine-Thomas-Par
	Tokyo Rose	Pine-Thomas-Par
	Deadline for Murder	Wurtzel-20th
	Swamp Fire	Pine-Thomas-Par
1947	*The Guilty*	Wrather-Mon
	Fear in the Night	Pine-Thomas-Par
	Gunfighters	Producers-Actors-Col
	(AC: Carbonara; O: Gilbert)	
	High Tide	Wrather-Mon
	Roses Are Red	Wurtzel-20th
1948	*Sleep, My Love*	Triangle-UA
	The Dangerous Years	Wurtzel-20th
	Perilous Waters	Wrather-Mon
	Coroner Creek	Producers-Actors-Col
	Strike It Rich	Wrather-AA
1949	*The Green Promise*	McCarthy-RKO
	The Great Dan Patch	Frank-UA
1950	*The Eagle and the Hawk*	Pine-Thomas-Par
	The Iroquois Trail	Small-UA
	High Lonesome (AC: Carbonara)	Lemay-Templeton-EL

WALTER SCHUMANN

1947 *Buck Privates Come Home* (O: Tamkin)   UI
      The Wistful Widow of Wagon Gap (O: Tamkin)   UI
1948 *The Noose Hangs High* (O: A. Morton)   EL
1949 *Africa Screams*   Nassour-UA

NATHAN SCOTT

1946 *Rendezvous with Annie* (with Dubin)   Republic
      Out California Way   Republic
1947 *Robin Hood of Texas*   Republic
      Wyoming (with Gold)   Republic
      Driftwood   Republic
1948 *Campus Honeymoon* (orchestration)   Republic
      The Inside Story   Republic
      Angel in Exile   Republic
      Angel on the Amazon   Republic
      Grand Canyon Trail   Republic
1949 *Wake of the Red Witch**   Republic
      The Red Menace   Republic
      *Brimstone**   Republic
      *The Kid from Cleveland**   Republic
      *The Golden Stallion**   Republic
1950 *Singing Guns* (O: Arnaud, Wilson)   Republic
      *The Avengers**   Republic
      *Surrender**   Republic
      *Trail of Robinhood**   Republic
      *California Passage**   Republic
1952 *Lady Possessed**   Republic
      *Oklahoma Annie**   Republic
      *Hoodlum Empire**   Republic
      *Montana Belle**   RKO

ALBERT SENDREY

1951 *Father's Little Dividend*   MGM

ANDREA SETARO
SCORER:
1934 *Bolero* (with Lawrence; AC, C, O: Ralph Rainger,
         Leipold, Hand, Kopp, Kaun, Harry Revel) Paramount

---

* Orchestration: Stanley Wilson.

	The Old-Fashioned Way	Paramount
	(with Lawrence; AC, C, O: Leipold, Satterfield)	
	Belle of the Nineties	Paramount
	(with Lawrence; AC, C, O: Leipold, Satterfield, Jackson)	
1935	*Goin' to Town*	Paramount
	(with Wineland; C, O: Leipold, Satterfield, Hand, Reese, Roemheld, Bradshaw, Sharpe, Pasternacki)	
	College Scandal	Paramount
	(with Wineland; C, O: Hollander, Leipold, Satterfield)	

MUSICAL DIRECTION:

1940	*Mystery Sea Raider*	Paramount
1941	*Nothing But the Truth*	Paramount

NATHANIEL SHILKRET

1928	*Lilac Time*	First National
1936	*The Bohemian Girl*	Roach-MGM
	Mary of Scotland (O: De Packh)	RKO
	Swing Time (MD)	RKO
	Walking on Air	RKO
	The Big Game	RKO
	Winterset (O: De Packh)	RKO
	Smartest Girl in Town	RKO
1937	*That Girl from Paris* (MD)	RKO
	The Soldier and the Lady (O: De Packh)	RKO
	Border Cafe	RKO
	The Toast of New York	RKO
	Music for Madame (MD)	RKO
1939	*"... one-third of a nation ..."*	Paramount
1941	*Frank Buck's Jungle Cavalcade*	RKO
	Stolen Paradise	Monogram
1943	*A Stranger in Town* (with Amfitheatrof)	MGM
	Air Raid Wardens	MGM
1944	*Three Men in White*	MGM
1945	*Blonde Fever*	MGM
	This Man's Navy	MGM
	Nothing But Trouble	MGM
	She Went to the Races	MGM
1946	*The Hoodlum Saint* (O: Sendrey)	MGM
	Boys' Ranch (O: Sendrey)	MGM
	Faithful in My Fashion (O: Sendrey)	MGM

SHORTS:

1932	*Puss-in-Boots*	Picture Classics

	Leningrad—the Gateway to Soviet Russia	**MGM**
	Rio the Magnificent	**MGM**
1933	*Beer Is Here*	Standard
	Cuba, the Land of Rhumba	**MGM**
	Iceland—Land of the Vikings	**MGM**
1934	*Ireland—the Emerald Isle*	**MGM**
1935	*George Washington's Railroad*	Ches. & Ohio
	Los Angeles—Wonder City of the West	**MGM**
1937	*Hongkong, the Hub of the Orient*	**MGM**
	Rocky Mountain Grandeur	**MGM**
	Serene Siam	**MGM**
1938	*Quintupland*	**RKO**
	Windward Way	Pathe
	Singapore and Jahore	**MGM**
	Sidney, Pride of Australia	**MGM**
1939	*Glimpses of Australia*	**MGM**
	Montmarte Madness	Columbia
	Yankee Doodle Home	Columbia
1942	*This Is America*	Pathe
1943	*Plan for Destruction*	**MGM**
	Heavenly Music (with Terr)	**MGM**
1944	*Ode to Victory*	**MGM**

Also several hundred other short subjects.

LEO SHUKEN

1937	*Waikiki Wedding*	Paramount
	(A, O: Franklin, Siegel, Young)	
1938	*Every Day's a Holiday* (arrangements)	Paramount
	Artists and Models Abroad	Paramount
1939	*Paris Honeymoon* (A: Franklin)	Paramount
	Cafe Society	Paramount
	Stagecoach	Wanger-UA
	(with Hageman, Harling, Leipold; AC: Carbonara)	
	The Lady from Kentucky	Wanger-UA
	The Flying Deuces (with Leipold)	RKO
1940	*Adventure in Diamonds*	Paramount
1941	*The Lady Eve* (with Bradshaw)	Paramount
	West Point Widow	Paramount
	Our Wife	Columbia
	New York Town	Paramount
1942	*Sullivan's Travels* (with Bradshaw)	Paramount
	The Lady Has Plans (with Harline)	Paramount
	Meet the Stewarts	Columbia
	Henry Aldrich, Editor	Paramount

1943	*The Good Fellows*	Paramount
	The Miracle of Morgan's Creek (with Bradshaw)	Paramount
1947	*The Fabulous Dorseys*	Rogers-UA
1949	*The Best Years* (Anniversary trailer; with Cutner)	MGM

LOUIS SILVERS

SCORE:

1920	*Way Down East* (with Peters)	Griffith-UA
1927	*The Jazz Singer* (O: Eddy Ross)	WB
1928	*Noah's Ark*	WB
1933	*Dancing Lady*	MGM

MUSICAL DIRECTION:

1933	*Stage Mother*	MGM
1934	*It Happened One Night* (O: Jackson)	Columbia
	Sisters Under the Skin	Columbia
	One Night of Love (O: Jackson)	Columbia
1935	*Love Me Forever*	Columbia
	Crime and Punishment	Columbia
1936	*Professional Soldier*	20th
	The Prisoner of Shark Island	20th
	The Country Doctor	20th
	A Message to Garcia	20th
	Captain January	20th
	Under Two Flags	20th
	Half Angel	20th
	Private Number	20th
	Sins of Man (A: Maxwell)	20th
	The Poor Little Rich Girl (MA: Mockridge)	20th
	To Mary—with Love	20th
	Sing, Baby, Sing	20th
	The Road to Glory	20th
	Ladies in Love	20th
	Dimples	20th
	Stowaway	20th
1937	*One in a Million* (A: Maxwell)	20th
	Lloyds of London	20th
	(AC, C, O: Mockridge, Bassett, Buttolph, Spencer)	
	Seventh Heaven	20th
	Wake Up and Live (O, A: Mockridge, Scharf,	
	Van Loan, Spencer, Rose, Virgil, Buttolph)	20th
	Cafe Metropole	20th
	Thin Ice (O, A: Bennett, Mockridge, Scharf, Spencer,	
	Maxwell, Van Loan, Buttolph, Rose)	20th

	Life Begins in College	20th
	Heidi (PS: Maxwell)	20th
	Ali Baba Goes to Town (O, A: Bennett, Rose, Sharpe, Buttolph, Mockridge, Spencer, Maxwell)	20th
	Love and Hisses	20th
1938	*Happy Landing*	20th
	The Baroness and the Butler	20th
	In Old Chicago (A: Maxwell)	20th
	Four Men and a Prayer	20th
	Kentucky Moonshine	20th
	Always Goodbye	20th
	I'll Give a Million	20th
	Little Miss Broadway	20th
	My Lucky Star	20th
	Straight, Place and Show	20th
	Suez (PS, A: Maxwell; PS: Raksin)	20th
	Just Around the Corner	20th
	Thanks for Everything (PS: Maxwell)	20th
	Kentucky	20th
1939	*Jesse James*	20th
	Tail Spin	20th
	The Little Princess (O: Spencer)	20th
	The Story of Alexander Graham Bell	20th
	Rose of Washington Square	20th
	Second Fiddle	20th
	Susannah of the Mounties (PS: Maxwell)	20th
	Stanley and Livingstone (PS: Bennett, Raksin)	20th
	Here I Am a Stranger	20th
	Hollywood Cavalcade	20th
1940	*Swanee River*	20th
1943	*The Powers Girl*	Rogers-UA

MARLIN SKILES

MUSICAL DIRECTION:

1937	*Great Guy*	Grand National
	23½ Hours Leave	Grand National
	Sweetheart of the Navy	Grand National
1944	*Kansas City Kitty*	Columbia
	Meet Miss Bobby Socks	Columbia
1946	*Gilda* (with Stoloff; PS, A: Arnaud)	Columbia

ARRANGEMENTS:

1945	*Tonight and Every Night*	Columbia

1946	*Tars and Spars*	Columbia
	(with Arnaud, S. Chaplin, Karger, Lane)	

SCORE:

1944	*Man from Frisco*	Republic
	The Impatient Years	Columbia
	Strange Affair	Columbia
1945	*A Thousand and One Nights*	Columbia
	Over 21	Columbia
	She Wouldn't Say Yes	Columbia
1946	*The Walls Came Tumbling Down*	Columbia
	Gallant Journey	Columbia
1947	*Dead Reckoning*	Columbia
	Framed	Columbia
1948	*Relentless*	Columbia
	Mickey	Seigel-EL
1950	*The Golden Gloves Story*	Central Natl.-EL
	The Great Wilderness (travelogue)	
1951	*The Lion Hunters*	Monogram
	Cavalry Scout	Monogram
	Flight to Mars	Monogram
	Callaway Went Thataway	MGM
1952	*Fort Osage*	Monogram
	Aladdin and His Lamp	Monogram
	Rodeo	Monogram
	Wild Stallion	Monogram
	Wagons West	Monogram
	The Rose Bowl Story	Monogram
	Army Bound	Monogram
	Battle Zone	Wanger-AA
	Flat Top	Monogram
	Hiawatha	Monogram

FRANK SKINNER

ORCHESTRATION:

1937	*Top of the Town*	Universal
	Merry-Go-Round of 1938	Universal
	You're a Sweetheart	Universal
1938	*Mad About Music*	Universal
	Youth Takes a Fling	Universal
	That Certain Age	Universal
	Swing, Sister, Swing	Universal
1939	*Three Smart Girls Grow Up*	Universal
	East Side of Heaven (with Trotter)	Universal

	First Love	Universal
	Tower of London	Universal
1940	It's a Date	Universal
	If I Had My Way	Universal
	Argentine Nights (with Schoen)	Universal
	The Boys from Syracuse	Universal
	Spring Parade (with Salter)	Universal
	A Little Bit of Heaven	Universal
	One Night in the Tropics	Universal
1941	Nice Girl?	Universal
	San Antonio Rose	Universal
	Moonlight in Hawaii	Universal
1943	It Ain't Hay	Universal
	Top Man	Universal
	Crazy House	Universal
1944	Chip Off the Old Block (with L. Russell)	Universal
	This Is the Life (with L. Russell)	Universal

SCORE:

1939	Son of Frankenstein	Universal
	The Sun Never Sets	Universal
	Charlie McCarthy, Detective	Universal
	Destry Rides Again	Universal
1940	The Invisible Man Returns (with Salter)	Universal
	My Little Chickadee	Universal
	The House of the Seven Gables	Universal
	When the Daltons Rode	Universal
	Hired Wife	Universal
	Seven Sinners (with Salter)	Universal
1941	Back Street	Universal
	The Lady from Cheyenne	Universal
	The Flame of New Orleans	Universal
	Never Give a Sucker an Even Break	Universal
	Appointment for Love	Universal
	Keep 'Em Flying	Universal
	Hellzapoppin'	Universal
1942	Jail House Blues	Universal
	Ride 'Em Cowboy	Universal
	Saboteur	Universal
	Broadway	Universal
	Lady in a Jam	Universal
	Eagle Squadron	Universal
	Sherlock Holmes and the Voice of Terror	Universal
	Who Done It?	Universal
	Pittsburgh (with Salter)	Universal
	Arabian Nights	Universal

1943	*Sherlock Holmes and the Secret Weapon*	Universal
	The Amazing Mrs. Holliday (with Salter)	Universal
	White Savage	Universal
	Sherlock Holmes in Washington	Universal
	Two Tickets to London	Universal
	Hers to Hold	Universal
	We've Never Been Licked	Universal
	Fired Wife	Universal
	Gung Ho!	Universal
1944	*Hi, Beautiful*	Universal
	Destiny (with Tansman)	Universal
1945	*The Suspect*	Universal
	Under Western Skies (MD)	Universal
	Blonde Ransom	Universal
	Strange Confession	Universal
	The Daltons Ride Again	Universal
	Pillow of Death	Universal
	Frontier Gal	Universal
1946	*Idea Girl*	Universal
	A Night in Paradise	Universal
	The Runaround	Universal
	Inside Job	Universal
	Canyon Passage	Universal
	Black Angel	Universal
1947	*Swell Guy**	UI
	*I'll Be Yours**	UI
	*The Egg and I**	UI
	*Ride the Pink Horse**	UI
	*The Exile**	UI
1948	*The Naked City* (with Rozsa; O: Zador)	UI
	Hazard (O: Cutner, Shuken)	Paramount
	*Abbott and Costello Meet Frankenstein**	UI
	*Tap Roots**	UI
	*For the Love of Mary**	UI
1949	*The Fighting O'Flynn**	UI
	*Family Honeymoon**	UI
	The Life of Riley	UI
	*Tulsa**	Wanger-EL
	The Lady Gambles	UI
	The Gal Who Took the West	UI
	Sword in the Desert	UI
	Free for All	UI
1950	*Woman in Hiding*	UI
	Francis	UI

---

* Orchestrations: David Tamkin.

	One Way Street	UI
	Comanche Territory	UI
	The Desert Hawk	UI
	Louisa	UI
	The Sleeping City	UI
	Harvey	UI
1951	*Bedtime for Bonzo*	UI
	Double Crossbones (O: Tamkin)	UI
	Katie Did It	UI
	Francis Goes to the Races	UI
	Mark of the Renegade	UI
	Bright Victory	UI
	The Lady Pays Off	UI
	The Raging Tide	UI
	Week End with Father	UI
1952	*No Room for the Groom*	UI
	Sally and Saint Anne	UI
	The World in His Arms	UI
	Bonzo Goes to College	UI
	Because of You	UI
	It Grows on Trees	UI
1953	*The Mississippi Gambler*	UI

PAUL SMITH

1938	*Snow White and the Seven Dwarfs* (with Churchill, Harline)	Disney-RKO
1940	*Pinocchio* (with Harline; O: Plumb, Stark, Wolcott)	Disney-RKO
1943	*Saludos Amigos* (with Plumb)	Disney-RKO
	Victory Through Air Power (with Plumb, Wallace; A: Fine, A. Morton, Stark, Vaughn)	Disney-UA
1944	*The Three Caballeros* (MD with Plumb, Wolcott)	Disney-RKO
1946	*Song of the South* (Cartoon only; photoplay score: Amfitheatrof; O: Plumb)	Disney-RKO
1947	*Fun and Fancy Free* (with Daniel, Wallace)	Disney-RKO
1948	*The Strange Mrs. Crane*	Sutherland-EL
	So Dear to My Heart (O: Plumb)	Disney-RKO
1950	*Cinderella* (MD with Wallace; O: Dubin, Plumb)	Disney-RKO
	Beaver Valley	Disney-RKO
1951	*Nature's Half Acre* (O: Plumb)	Disney-RKO

1952	*The Olympic Elk*	Disney-RKO
	Water Birds	Disney-RKO

Also many Disney cartoons.

DAVID SNELL

FEATURES:

1937	*Dangerous Number*	MGM
	A Family Affair	MGM
	The Thirteenth Chair	MGM
	Married Before Breakfast	MGM
	My Dear Miss Aldrich	MGM
	Madame X	MGM
	You're Only Young Once	MGM
1938	*Judge Hardy's Children*	MGM
	Love Finds Andy Hardy	MGM
	Young Dr. Kildare	MGM
	Out West with the Hardys	MGM
1939	*Burn 'Em Up O'Connor*	MGM
	The Hardys Ride High	MGM
	Calling Dr. Kildare	MGM
	Stronger Than Desire (with Ward)	MGM
	They All Come Out (with Ward)	MGM
	Andy Hardy Gets Spring Fever (with Ward)	MGM
	These Glamour Girls (with Ward; O: Heglin)	MGM
	The Women (with Ward; O: Heglin, Raab)	MGM
	Blackmail (with Ward)	MGM
	Thunder Afloat (with Ward)	MGM
	Dancing Co-ed (with Ward)	MGM
	The Secret of Dr. Kildare	MGM
	Joe and Ethel Turp Call on the President (with Ward)	MGM
	Henry Goes Arizona	MGM
	Judge Hardy and Son	MGM
1940	*The Man from Dakota* (with Amfitheatrof)	MGM
	The Ghost Comes Home	MGM
	Dr. Kildare's Strange Case	MGM
	20 Mule Team	MGM
	Phantom Raiders	MGM
	Andy Hardy Meets Debutante	MGM
	(A: Edens; O: Arnaud, Heglin, Salinger, Van Eps)	
	Gold Rush Maisie	MGM
	The Golden Fleecing	MGM
	Dr. Kildare Goes Home	MGM
	Wyoming	MGM
	Sky Murder	MGM
	Third Finger, Left Hand	MGM

	Gallant Sons	MGM
	Dr. Kildare's Crisis	MGM
1941	*Maisie Was a Lady*	MGM
	Wild Man of Borneo	MGM
	The Penalty	MGM
	Washington Melodrama	MGM
	The People vs. Dr. Kildare	MGM
	Love Crazy	MGM
	Billy the Kid	MGM
	Ringside Maisie	MGM
	Down in San Diego	MGM
	Unholy Partners	MGM
	Shadow of the Thin Man	MGM
	Tarzan's Secret Treasure	MGM
1942	*Mr. and Mrs. North*	MGM
	The Vanishing Virginian (MA: Brent)	MGM
	Born to Sing (MD with Hayton; O: Heglin, Raab)	MGM
	The Courtship of Andy Hardy	MGM
	Kid Glove Killer	MGM
	Tarzan's New York Adventure	MGM
	Grand Central Murder	MGM
	Pacific Rendezvous	MGM
	Jackass Mail (AC: Brent)	MGM
	Tish	MGM
	The War Against Mrs. Hadley	MGM
	The Omaha Trail	MGM
1943	*Northwest Rangers* (with Amfitheatrof)	MGM
	The Youngest Profession	MGM
	The Man from Down Under	MGM
1944	*Rationing* (AC: Kaplan)	MGM
	See Here, Private Hargrove	MGM
	Swing Fever	MGM
	(MD with Stoll; A: Brent; O: Duning, Heglin, Moore)	
	Andy Hardy's Blonde Trouble	MGM
	Barbary Coast Gent	MGM
	Maisie Goes to Reno	MGM
	Lost in a Harem (MD; O: Burke, Duncan, Heglin)	MGM
1945	*The Thin Man Goes Home*	MGM
	Between Two Women	MGM
	Keep Your Powder Dry	MGM
	Gentle Annie	MGM
	Twice Blessed (MD; A: Brent; O: Heglin)	MGM
	The Hidden Eye	MGM
	Dangerous Partners	MGM
	What Next, Corporal Hargrove?	MGM
1946	*Up Goes Maisie* (O: Duncan, Franklyn, Heglin)	MGM

	Bad Bascomb (PS, O: Franklyn; O: Heglin)	MGM
	The Cockeyed Miracle	MGM
	The Show-Off (O: Heglin)	MGM
1947	*The Mighty McGurk* (O: Heglin)	MGM
	Lady in the Lake	MGM
	Love Laughs at Andy Hardy (O: Heglin)	MGM
	Undercover Maisie	MGM
	Dark Delusion	MGM
	Song of the Thin Man	MGM
	Merton of the Movies	MGM
	Killer McCoy	MGM
1948	*Alias a Gentleman*	MGM
	A Southern Yankee	MGM

SHORTS:

1935	*Windy*	MGM
1936	*How to Behave*	MGM
1937	*Bars and Stripes*	MGM
	Some Time Soon	MGM
	Carnival in Paris	MGM
	Song of Revolt	MGM
1938	*The Canary Comes Across*	MGM
	An Optical Poem	MGM
	(MA of Liszt's 2nd Hungarian Rhapsody; O: Marquardt)	
	That Mothers Might Live	MGM
	The Forgotten Step	MGM
	Snow Gets in Your Eyes	MGM
	Joaquin Murrieta	MGM
	Tupapaoo	MGM
	The Giant of Norway	MGM
	Strange Glory	MGM
	Tracking the Sleeping Death	MGM
	The Magician's Daughter	MGM
	It's in the Stars	MGM
	The Man on the Rock	MGM
	Aladdin's Lantern	MGM
	Nostradamus	MGM
	John Nesbit's Passing Parade	MGM
	Men in Fright	MGM
	They Live Again	MGM
	The Miracle of Salt Lake	MGM
	Men of Steel	MGM
	Once Over Lightly	MGM
	The Great Heart	MGM
1939	*Electrical Power*	MGM
	Ice Antics	MGM

The Story of Alfred Nobel	**MGM**
Tiny Troubles	**MGM**
The Story of Dr. Jenner	**MGM**
Somewhat Secret	**MGM**
Happily Buried	**MGM**
Angel of Mercy	**MGM**
Prophet Without Honor	**MGM**
Yankee Doodle Goes to Town	**MGM**
The Story That Couldn't Be Printed	**MGM**
Captain Spanky's Show Boat	**MGM**
Football Thrills of 1938	**MGM**

WILLY STAHL

1944	*Timber Queen*	Pine-Thomas-Par
	The Navy Way	Pine-Thomas-Par
	Dark Mountain	Pine-Thomas-Par

RALPH STANLEY

1947	*The Burning Cross*	Somerset-SG
1948	*Let's Live Again*	Seltzer-20th
	The Argyle Secrets	Eronel-FC
	Shed No Tears	Equity-EL
	The Gay Intruders	Seltzer-20th
	Night Wind	Wurtzel-20th
	Unknown Island	Cohen-FC
	Strange Gamble	Cassidy-UA
1950	*Timber Fury*	Schwarz-EL
	Roll, Thunder, Roll	Equity-EL

MAX STEINER

1929	*Rio Rita* (orchestration)	RKO
1930	*Dixiana* (orchestration)	RKO
	Half Shot at Sunrise	RKO
1931	*Beau Ideal*	RKO
	Cimarron	RKO
	Kept Husbands	RKO
	Transgression	RKO
	Travelling Husbands	RKO
	The Gay Diplomat	RKO
	Consolation Marriage	RKO

	Are These Our Children?	RKO
1932	*The Lost Squadron*	RKO
	Symphony of Six Million	RKO
	Westward Passage	RKO
	Is My Face Red?	RKO
	What Price Hollywood	RKO
	Roar of the Dragon	RKO
	Bird of Paradise	RKO
	The Most Dangerous Game	RKO
	Thirteen Women	RKO
	A Bill of Divorcement	RKO
	Little Orphan Annie	RKO
	The Sport Parade	RKO
	The Conquerors	RKO
	Rockabye	RKO
	The Half Naked Truth	RKO
	The Animal Kingdom	RKO
1933	*No Other Woman*	RKO
	The Monkey's Paw	RKO
	Cheyenne Kid	RKO
	Lucky Devils	RKO
	Topaze	RKO
	The Great Jaspar	RKO
	So This Is Harris (short)	RKO
	Our Betters	RKO
	Christopher Strong	RKO
	King Kong	RKO
	Sweepings	RKO
	Diplomaniacs	RKO
	The Silver Cord	RKO
	Emergency Call	RKO
	Melody Cruise	RKO
	Bed of Roses	RKO
	Flying Devils	RKO
	Double Harness	RKO
	Headline Shooter	RKO
	Before Dawn	RKO
	No Marriage Ties	RKO
	Morning Glory	RKO
	Blind Adventure	RKO
	Rafter Romance	RKO
	One Man's Journey	RKO
	Midshipman Jack	RKO
	Ann Vickers	RKO
	Ace of Aces	RKO
	Chance at Heaven	RKO

	Aggie Appleby, Maker of Men	RKO
	After Tonight	RKO
	The Right to Romance	RKO
	Little Women	RKO
	If I Were Free	RKO
	Son of Kong	RKO
	Flying Down to Rio (MD)	RKO
1934	*The Meanest Gal in Town*	RKO
	Long Lost Father	RKO
	Two Alone	RKO
	Hips, Hips, Hooray! (MD)	RKO
	Man of Two Worlds	RKO
	The Lost Patrol	RKO
	Keep 'Em Rolling	RKO
	Success at Any Price	RKO
	Spitfire	RKO
	This Man Is Mine	RKO
	Sing and Like It	RKO
	The Crime Doctor	RKO
	Finishing School	RKO
	Where Sinners Meet	RKO
	Stingaree	RKO
	Strictly Dynamite	RKO
	Murder on the Blackboard	RKO
	The Life of Vergie Winters	RKO
	Let's Try Again	RKO
	We're Rich Again	RKO
	Of Human Bondage	RKO
	Bachelor Bait	RKO
	His Greatest Gamble	RKO
	Their Big Moment	RKO
	Hat, Coat and Glove	RKO
	The Fountain	RKO
	Down to Their Last Yacht (MD)	RKO
	The Age of Innocence	RKO
	The Richest Girl in the World	RKO
	Dangerous Corner	RKO
	The Gay Divorcee (MD)	RKO
	Wednesday's Child	RKO
	Gridiron Flash	RKO
	By Your Leave	RKO
	Anne of Green Gables	RKO
	The Silver Streak	RKO
	The Little Minister	RKO
1935	*West of the Pecos*	RKO
	Roberta (MD)	RKO

	Star of Midnight	RKO
	The Informer	RKO
	Break of Hearts	RKO
	She	RKO
	Alice Adams	RKO
	Top Hat (MD; O: Powell)	RKO
	The Three Musketeers	RKO
	I Dream Too Much (MD; O: Bennett)	RKO
1936	*Follow the Fleet* (MD)	RKO
	Little Lord Fauntleroy	Selznick-UA
	The Charge of the Light Brigade (F)	WB
	The Garden of Allah	Selznick-UA
1937	*God's Country and the Woman* (F)	WB
	Green Light (F)	WB
	A Star Is Born	Selznick-UA
	Kid Galahad (F)	WB
	Slim (F)	WB
	That Certain Woman (F)	WB
	The Life of Emile Zola (F)	WB
	Submarine D-1 (F)	WB
	First Lady (F)	WB
	Tovarich	WB
1938	*Gold Is Where You Find It* (F)	WB
	Jezebel (F)	WB
	Crime School (F)	WB
	White Banners	WB
	The Amazing Dr. Clitterhouse	WB
	Four Daughters (F)	WB
	The Sisters (F)	WB
	Angels with Dirty Faces (F)	WB
	The Dawn Patrol (F)	WB
1939	*They Made Me a Criminal* (F)	WB
	The Oklahoma Kid (F&D)	WB
	Dodge City (F)	WB
	Dark Victory (F)	WB
	Confessions of a Nazi Spy	WB
	Daughters Courageous (H)	WB
	Each Dawn I Die (F)	WB
	The Old Maid (F)	WB
	Dust Be My Destiny (F)	WB
	We Are Not Alone (F)	WB
	Four Wives (F&H)	WB
	Gone with the Wind	Selznick-MGM
1940	*The Story of Dr. Ehrlich's Magic Bullet* (F)	WB
	Virginia City (F)	WB
	All This, and Heaven Too (F)	WB

	City for Conquest (F)	WB
	A Dispatch from Reuter's (F)	WB
	The Letter (F)	WB
	Santa Fe Trail (F)	WB
1941	*The Great Lie* (F&H)	WB
	Shining Victory (F)	WB
	The Bride Came C.O.D. (F)	WB
	Dive Bomber (F)	WB
	Sergeant York (F)	WB
	One Foot in Heaven (F)	WB
1942	*They Died with Their Boots On*	WB
	Captains of the Clouds	WB
	In This Our Life (F)	WB
	The Gay Sisters (F)	WB
	Desperate Journey (F)	WB
	Now, Voyager (F)	WB
1943	*Casablanca* (F)	WB
	Mission to Moscow (K)	WB
	Watch on the Rhine (F)	WB
1944	*Passage to Marseille*	WB
	The Adventures of Mark Twain (K)	WB
	Since You Went Away	Selznick-UA
	Arsenic and Old Lace (F)	WB
	The Conspirators (R; AC: Friedhofer)	WB
1945	*Roughly Speaking* (F)	WB
	The Corn Is Green (F)	WB
	Mildred Pierce (F)	WB
	Tomorrow Is Forever	International-RKO
	San Antonio (F)	WB
1946	*My Reputation*	WB
	Saratoga Trunk (K)	WB
	One More Tomorrow	WB
	A Stolen Life (F)	WB
	The Big Sleep	WB
	Cloak and Dagger (F)	WB
1947	*The Man I Love* (F)	WB
	The Beast with Five Fingers (F)	WB
	Pursued (C)	WB
	Love and Learn (C&H)	WB
	Cheyenne (F)	WB
	The Unfaithful (C)	WB
	Deep Valley (C)	WB
	Life with Father (C)	WB
1948	*The Treasure of the Sierra Madre* (C)	WB
	My Girl Tisa	WB
	The Voice of the Turtle (C)	WB

	Winter Meeting (C)	WB
	The Woman in White (C)	WB
	Silver River (C)	WB
	Key Largo (C)	WB
	Johnny Belinda (C)	WB
	Fighter Squadron (C)	WB
	The Decision of Christopher Blake (C)	WB
1949	*Adventures of Don Juan* (C)	WB
	South of St. Louis (C)	WB
	A Kiss in the Dark (C)	WB
	Flamingo Road (C)	WB
	The Fountainhead (C)	WB
	White Heat (C)	WB
	Without Honor (C)	Hakim-UA
	Beyond the Forest (C)	WB
	Mrs. Mike	Regal-UA
	The Lady Takes a Sailor (C)	WB
1950	*Caged* (C)	WB
	The Flame and the Arrow (C)	WB
	The Glass Menagerie (C)	WB
	Rocky Mountain (C)	WB
	Dallas (C)	WB
1951	*Operation Pacific* (C)	WB
	Sugarfoot (C)	WB
	Lightning Strikes Twice (C)	WB
	Raton Pass	WB
	Jim Thorpe—All-American (C)	WB
	Force of Arms (C)	WB
	Close to My Heart (C)	WB
	Distant Drums (C)	WB
1952	*Room for One More* (C)	WB
	The Lion and the Horse (C)	WB
	Mara Maru (C)	WB
	The Miracle of Our Lady of Fatima (C)	WB
	Springfield Rifle (C)	WB
	The Iron Mistress (C)	WB

Note: Letters in parentheses following some titles indicate orchestrators: (C) Murray Cutter; (D) Adolph Deutsch; (F) Hugo Friedhofer; (H) Ray Heindorf; (K) Bernard Kaun; (R) Leonid Raab.

ALEXANDER STEINERT

Radio Operator	A.A.F.
Camouflage	A.A.F.
Target for Today	A.A.F.

1946	*Strangler of the Swamp*	PRC
	Devil Bat's Daughter	PRC
	The Unknown	Columbia
	Personality Kid	Columbia
	Little Iodine	Comet-UA
	Blondie Knows Best	Columbia
	Don Ricardo Returns	PRC
1948	*The Prairie*	Zenith-SG

LEITH STEVENS

1942	*Syncopation*	RKO
1948	*Night Song*	RKO
	Black Bart (Music for dances: Skinner)	UI
	All My Sons (O: Tamkin)	UI
	Feudin', Fussin' and A-Fightin'	UI
	Larceny	UI
1949	*Not Wanted*	Emerald-FC
1950	*Never Fear* (O: Torbett)	Filmakers-EL
	The Great Rupert (O: Wheeler)	Pal-EL
	Destination Moon (O: Torbett)	Pal-EL
1951	*The Sun Sets at Dawn*	Holiday-EL
	No Questions Asked	MGM
	When Worlds Collide (O: Cutner, Shuken)	Pal-Par
1952	*Navajo* (doc.)	Bartlett-Lippert
	The Atomic City	Paramount
	Storm Over Tibet (AC; score: Honegger)	Summit-Col
	Beware, My Lovely	RKO
	Eight Iron Men	Kramer-Col

WILLIAM GRANT STILL

PART SCORE:

1936	*Lady of Secrets*	Columbia
	Theodora Goes Wild	Columbia
	Pennies from Heaven	Columbia

Also composed about 29 sketches for the stock catalogue at Columbia.

GEORGIE STOLL

MUSICAL DIRECTION:

| 1936 | *Swing Banditry* (short) | MGM |

1937	*Broadway Melody of 1938*	MGM

1937 *Broadway Melody of 1938* MGM
  (A: Edens; O: Arnaud, Cutter)
1938 *Radio City Revels* RKO
1939 *Ice Follies of 1939* MGM
  (with Waxman; score: Edens; O: Arnaud, Bassman)
  Babes in Arms (MA: Edens; O: Arnaud, Bassman) MGM
1940 *Two Girls on Broadway* MGM
  (A: Ruick; O: Arnaud, Bassman)
  Forty Little Mothers MGM
  (A: Edens; O: Bassman, Heglin)
  Strike Up the Band (O: Arnaud, Salinger) MGM
  Hullabaloo MGM
  (O: Arnaud, Bassman, Marquardt, Van Eps)
  Little Nellie Kelly (MA: Edens) MGM
  Go West (O: Bassman) MGM
1941 *Road Show* (score) Roach-UA
  The Big Store MGM
  (MA: Brent; O: Arnaud, Bassman, Taylor, Van Eps)
  Life Begins for Andy Hardy MGM
  Lady Be Good MGM
  (continuity: Ruick; O: Arnaud, Bassman, Salinger)
1942 *Babes on Broadway* MGM
  (MA: Edens; O: Arnaud, Bassman, Salinger)
  Ship Ahoy MGM
  (O: Arnaud, Bassman, Oliver, Salinger, Stordahl)
  Panama Hattie MGM
  (MA: Edens; O: Arnaud, Bassman, Salinger)
  For Me and My Gal MGM
  (MA: Edens; O: Arnaud, Bassman, Salinger)
1943 *Cabin in the Sky* (MA: Edens; O: Bassman) MGM
  Presenting Lily Mars (MA: Edens) MGM
  Du Barry Was a Lady MGM
  (MA: Edens; O: Arnaud, Bassman, Oliver, Stordahl)
  I Dood It MGM
  Girl Crazy MGM
  (MA: Edens; O: Oliver, Salinger, Stordahl)
1944 *Swing Fever* MGM
  (with Snell; A: Brent; O: Duning, Heglin, Moore)
  Two Girls and a Sailor MGM
1945 *Meet Me in St. Louis* MGM
  (MA: Edens; O, PS: Salinger)
  Music for Millions (MA; incidental MGM
  music: Michelet; O: Duncan, Jackson, Nussbaum)
  Thrill of a Romance (MA; O: Cutner, Duncan, Jackson,
  Norman, Nussbaum, Salinger, Winterhalter) MGM
  Anchors Aweigh (O: Stordahl) MGM

	Her Highness and the Bellboy	MGM
	(score; O: Cutner, Jackson, Shuken)	
1946	*Holiday in Mexico*	MGM
	(O: Duncan, Marquardt, Nussbaum, Schwandt)	
	No Leave, No Love (O: Bergman, Byrns,	MGM
	Duncan, Franklyn, Jackson, Nussbaum, Sendrey)	
1947	*This Time for Keeps* (O: Byrns, Jackson, Sendrey)	MGM
1948	*Big City* (O: Arnaud)	MGM
	On an Island with You (PS, O: Sendrey)	MGM
	A Date with Judy	MGM
	(O: Arnaud, Franklyn; PS, O: Sendrey)	
	Luxury Liner	MGM
1949	*The Kissing Bandit* (O: Arnaud; PS, O: Sendrey)	MGM
	Neptune's Daughter (O: Arnaud)	MGM
	In the Good Old Summertime (O: Salinger)	MGM
1950	*Nancy Goes to Rio* (O: Sendrey)	MGM
	Duchess of Idaho (O: Martin; PS, O: Sendrey)	MGM
	The Toast of New Orleans	MGM
	(O: Arnaud, Franklyn, Salinger, Sendrey)	
	Two Weeks with Love	MGM
	(O: Arnaud, Martin, Salinger; PS, O: Sendrey)	
1951	*Watch the Birdie* (score; O, AC: Sendrey)	MGM
	Excuse My Dust (O: Arnaud, Martin)	MGM
	The Strip (O: Arnaud, Rugolo)	MGM
1952	*Skirts Ahoy!* (O: Rugolo; PS, O: Sendrey)	MGM
	Glory Alley (O: Rugolo; PS, O: Sendrey)	MGM

GREGORY STONE

1936	*Easy to Take*	Paramount
1937	*Internes Can't Take Money*	Paramount
1938	*Her Jungle Love* (A: Roder)	Paramount
	Girl's School	Columbia
	Ride a Crooked Mile	Paramount
1940	*Her First Romance*	Chadwick-Mon

HERBERT STOTHART

1930	*Devil May Care* (Ballet music: Tiomkin)	MGM
	Montana Moon	MGM
	The Rogue Song (Ballet music: Tiomkin)[1]	MGM
	In Gay Madrid	MGM

[1] Arrangements: Charles Maxwell.

	The Floradora Girl	MGM
	Call of the Flesh	MGM
	Madam Satan[1]	MGM
	A Lady's Morals	MGM
1931	*New Moon*[1]	MGM
	The Prodigal[1]	MGM
	The Squaw Man	MGM
	The Cuban Love Song[2]	MGM
1932	*The Son-Daughter*[1]	MGM
1933	*Rasputin and the Empress*[1]	MGM
	The White Sister[1]	MGM
	The Barbarian[1]	MGM
	Peg o' My Heart[1]	MGM
	Turn Back the Clock	MGM
	Night Flight[2]	MGM
	Going Hollywood	MGM
1934	*Queen Christina*	MGM
	The Cat and the Fiddle (MD)	MGM
	Riptide	MGM
	Laughing Boy	MGM
	Viva Villa! (O: Allen, de Packh, Marquardt, Snell)[2]	MGM
	Treasure Island[1]	MGM
	Chained	MGM
	The Barretts of Wimpole Street	MGM
	What Every Woman Knows	MGM
	The Merry Widow (MA)[1]	MGM
	The Painted Veil[1]	MGM
	The Spectacle Maker (short)	MGM
1935	*Biography of a Bachelor Girl*	MGM
	The Night Is Young (MD)	MGM
	David Copperfield[2]	MGM
	Sequoia[1]	MGM
	Vanessa, Her Love Story	MGM
	Naughty Marietta (MA; O: Marquardt)[1]	MGM
	China Seas	MGM
	Anna Karenina[1]	MGM
	Mutiny on the Bounty[1]	MGM
	A Night at the Opera	MGM
	Ah, Wilderness!	MGM
	A Tale of Two Cities[2]	MGM
1936	*Rose Marie* (MD)[1]	MGM
	Wife vs. Secretary (with Ward)	MGM
	Moonlight Murder (with Ward)	MGM

[1]Arrangements: Charles Maxwell.
[2]Arrangements and part score: Maxwell.

	Small Town Girl (with Ward)	MGM
	The Robin Hood of El Dorado[1]	MGM
	Master Will Shakespeare (short)	MGM
	San Francisco (MD)[1]	MGM
	The Gorgeous Hussy	MGM
	The Devil Is a Sissy	MGM
	After the Thin Man (with Ward)	MGM
1937	*Camille*	MGM
	Maytime (MA, MD; O: Marquardt)	MGM
	Romeo and Juliet	MGM
	The Good Earth (O: Raab)	MGM
	Conquest (O: Arnaud, Cutter, Marquardt, Raab)	
	The Firefly (MD)	MGM
	Rosalie	MGM
	(MD; O: Arnaud, Cutter, Marquardt, Raab)	
1938	*Of Human Hearts*	MGM
	The Girl of the Golden West	MGM
	(MD; O: Arnaud, Cutter, Marquardt, Raab)	
	Marie Antoinette (O: Cutter)	MGM
	Sweethearts (MA; O: Cutter, Marquardt)	MGM
1939	*Idiot's Delight*	MGM
	Broadway Serenade (with Ward; O: Arnaud, Raab)	MGM
	The Wizard of Oz	
	(MA; O: Arnaud, Bassman, Cutter, Marquardt)	MGM
	Balalaika (O: Cutter, Heglin, Marquardt)	MGM
1940	*Northwest Passage*	MGM
	(O: Amfitheatrof, Cutter, Marquardt, Maxwell, Raab)	
	Edison, the Man	MGM
	Waterloo Bridge	MGM
	Susan and God	MGM
	New Moon (MD; O: Cutter)	MGM
	Pride and Prejudice	MGM
	Bitter Sweet (MD)	MGM
1941	*Come Live with Me*	MGM
	Andy Hardy's Private Secretary	MGM
	Men of Boys Town	MGM
	Ziegfeld Girl (O: Arnaud, Bassman, Salinger)	MGM
	They Met in Bombay	MGM
	Blossoms in the Dust	MGM
	Smilin' Through (MD)	MGM
	The Chocolate Soldier (MA, MD with Kaper)	MGM
1942	*Rio Rita* (MD; O: Arnaud, Cutter, Marquardt)	MGM
	I Married an Angel	MGM
	Mrs. Miniver	MGM

---

[1] Arrangements: Charles Maxwell.

STOTHART *(Continued)*

	Cairo	MGM
1943	*Tennessee Johnson*	MGM
	Three Hearts for Julia	MGM
	Random Harvest	MGM
	The Human Comedy	MGM
1944	*Thousands Cheer* (MD)	MGM
	Madame Curie	MGM
	Song of Russia (MA)	MGM
	A Guy Named Joe	MGM
	The White Cliffs of Dover	MGM
	Dragon Seed	MGM
	Kismet	MGM
1945	*Thirty Seconds Over Toyko*	MGM
	National Velvet	MGM
	The Picture of Dorian Gray	MGM
	The Valley of Decision	MGM
	Son of Lassie (O: Cutter, Franklyn)	MGM
	They Were Expendable	MGM
1946	*Adventure* (O: Cutter)	MGM
	The Green Years	MGM
	Undercurrent (O: Sendrey)	MGM
1947	*The Sea of Grass* (O: Sendrey)	MGM
	The Yearling	MGM
	(Themes by Delius; O: Bassett, Byrns, Heglin, Sendrey)	
	High Barbaree (O: Sendrey)	MGM
	The Unfinished Dance (O: Sendrey)	MGM
	Desire Me (O: Sendrey)	MGM
1948	*If Winter Comes*	MGM
	Three Daring Daughters	MGM
	The Three Musketeers	MGM
	(Themes by Tchaikovsky; O, AC: Sendrey)	
	Hills of Home (O: Franklyn, Sendrey)	MGM
1949	*Big Jack*	MGM

ALEXANDRE TANSMAN

1943	*Flesh and Fantasy*	Universal
1944	*Destiny* (with Skinner)	Universal
1945	*Paris—Underground*	Bennett-UA
1946	*Sister Kenny*	RKO

DEEMS TAYLOR

1924	*Janice Meredith*	Metro-Goldwyn

VIRGIL THOMSON

1936	*The Plow That Broke the Plains*	Resettlement Administration
1937	*The Spanish Earth*	Contemporary Historians
	(music arranged with Marc Blitzstein)	
1937	*The River*	Farm Security Administration
1945	*A Tuesday in November*	
1948	*Louisiana Story*	Robert Flaherty

DIMITRI TIOMKIN

1930	*Lord Byron of Broadway* (Ballet music)	MGM
	Devil May Care (Ballet music)	MGM
	The Rogue Song (Ballet music)	MGM
1931	*Resurrection*	Universal
1933	*Alice in Wonderland*	Paramount
	(scorers: Setaro, Lawrence; AC, C, O:	
	Leipold, Reese, Potoker, Hand, Jackson)	
1934	*Roast Beef and Movies* (short)	MGM
1935	*The Casino Murder Case*	MGM
	Mad Love	MGM
	I Live My Life	MGM
1937	*The Road Back* (A: Maxwell)	Universal
	Lost Horizon (A, O: Maxwell)	Columbia
1938	*Spawn of the North*	Paramount
	(AC, A: Carbonara, Harling, Roder)	
	You Can't Take It With You	Columbia
	The Great Waltz (MA, A)	MGM
1939	*Mr. Smith Goes to Washington*	Columbia
1940	*Lucky Partners*	RKO
	The Westerner	Goldwyn-UA
1941	*Meet John Doe*	Capra-WB
	Forced Landing	Paramount
	Scattergood Meets Broadway	RKO
	Flying Blind	Paramount
	The Corsican Brothers	Small-UA
1942	*A Gentleman After Dark*	Small-UA
	Twin Beds	Small-UA
	The Moon and Sixpence	Loew-Lewin-UA
1943	*Shadow of a Doubt*	Universal
	The Unknown Guest	Monogram
1944	*The Bridge of San Luis Rey*	Bogeaus-UA
	The Imposter	Universal
	Ladies Courageous	Universal
	When Strangers Marry	Monogram
1945	*Forever Yours*	Monogram
	Dillinger	Monogram

	China's Little Devils	Monogram
	Pardon My Past	Mutual-Col
1946	*Whistle Stop* (O: Gilbert)	Nero-UA
	Black Beauty	Alson-20th
	Angel on My Shoulder	Rogers-UA
	The Dark Mirror	UI
1947	*It's a Wonderful Life* (O: Gilbert)	Liberty-RKO
	Duel in the Sun (O: Gilbert)	Selznick-SRO
	The Long Night	Hakim-Litvak-RKO
1948	*Tarzan and the Mermaids*	Lesser-RKO
	So This Is New York	Kramer-UA
	The Dude Goes West	King Bros.-AA
	Red River	Monterey-UA
1949	*Portrait of Jennie* (Themes by Debussy)	Selznick-SRO
	Canadian Pacific	Holt-20th
	Champion	Kramer-UA
	Home of the Brave	Kramer-UA
	Red Light	Del Ruth-UA
1950	*Guilty Bystander*	Laurel-FC
	Dakota Lil	Alson-20th
	Champagne for Caesar	Popkin-UA
	D.O.A.	Popkin-UA
	The Men	Kramer-UA
	Cyrano de Bergerac	Kramer-UA
1951	*Mr. Universe*	Laurel-ELC
	The Thing	Winchester-RKO
	Strangers on a Train	WB
	Peking Express (O: Cutner, Shuken)	Paramount
	The Well	Popkin-UA
	Drums in the Deep South	King Bros.-RKO
1952	*Bugles in the Afternoon*	Cagney-WB
	Mutiny	King Bros.-UA
	My Six Convicts	Kramer-Col
	Lady in the Iron Mask	Wanger-Frenke-20th
	High Noon	Kramer-UA
	The Big Sky	Winchester-RKO
	The Steel Trap	Thor-20th
	The Happy Time	Kramer-Col
1953	*The Four Poster*	Kramer-Col
	Angel Face	RKO
	Jeopardy	MGM
	I Confess	WB

DOCUMENTARIES:

1942	*Moscow Strikes Back*	Artkino-Rep

1942-1945, for U. S. War Dept. (later Army Pictorial Service):

119

TIOMKIN *(Continued)*

Prelude to War, The Nazis Strike, Divide and Conquer, The Battle of Britain, The Battle of Russia, The Battle of China, War Comes to America, Know Your Enemy: Germany, Know Your Enemy: Japan, Know Your Ally: Britain, The Battle of Tunisia, San Pietro, The Negro Soldier, Substitution and Conversion, Two Down—One to Go, Operation Titantic, Tunisian Victory (with William Alwyn).

ERNST TOCH

1934	*Catherine the Great*	London Films-UA
	The Private Life of Don Juan	London Films-UA
	Little Friend	Gaumont-British
1935	*Peter Ibbetson* (AC: Harling)	Paramount
1937	*Outcast*	Paramount
	On Such a Night	Paramount
1939	*The Cat and the Canary*	Paramount
1940	*Dr. Cyclops* (with Carbonara, Malotte)	Paramount
	The Ghost Breakers	Paramount
1941	*Ladies in Retirement*	Columbia
1943	*First Comes Courage*	Columbia
1944	*None Shall Escape*	Columbia
	Address Unknown (AC: Castelnuovo-Tedesco)	Columbia
1945	*The Unseen*	Paramount

VAN CLEAVE

	Champagne for Two (short)	Paramount
1948	*The 'Sainted' Sisters*	Paramount
1950	*Dear Wife* (with Lilley)	Paramount
	Fancy Pants (O: Cutner, Parrish, Plumb, Shuken)	Paramount
1951	*Molly*	Paramount
	Quebec (with Plumb)	Paramount
	Dear Brat	Paramount
	Rhubarb (O: Cutner, Shuken)	Paramount

OLIVER WALLACE

1941	*Dumbo* (with Churchill; O: Plumb)	Disney-RKO
1943	*Victory Through Air Power*	Disney-UA
	(with Plumb, Smith; A: Fine, A. Morton, Stark, Vaughn)	
1947	*Fun and Fancy Free* (with Daniel, Smith)	Disney-RKO

1949	*The Adventures of Ichabod and Mr. Toad* (MD; O: Dubin)	Disney-RKO
1950	*Cinderella* (MD with Smith; O: Dubin, Plumb)	Disney-RKO
	Seal Island (O: Dubin, Stark)	Disney-RKO
1951	*Alice in Wonderland* (O: Dubin)	Disney-RKO
1953	*Peter Pan* (O: Plumb)	Disney-RKO

Also many Disney cartoons.

EDWARD WARD

1929	*Paris* (O: Satterfield)	WB
	Show of Shows	WB
1930	*Wedding Rings*	WB
	Song of the Flame	WB
	Bride of the Regiment	WB
1931	*Kismet*	WB
1932	*Hypnotized*	World Wide
1934	*I Like It That Way*	Universal
	Embarrassing Moments	Universal
	Romance in the Rain	Universal
	Gift of Gab	Universal
	Great Expectations	Universal
	Cheating Cheaters	Universal
	Girl o' My Dreams	Monogram
1935	*Mystery of Edwin Drood*	Universal
	Times Square Lady	MGM
	Reckless	MGM
	Age of Indiscretion	MGM
	Public Hero No. 1	MGM
	No More Ladies	MGM
	Here Comes the Band	MGM
	The Bishop Misbehaves	MGM
	Kind Lady	MGM
1936	*Riff Raff*	MGM
	Exclusive Story	MGM
	Wife vs. Secretary (with Stothart)	MGM
	Moonlight Murder (with Stothart)	MGM
	Small Town Girl (with Stothart)	MGM
	Speed	MGM
	Women Are Trouble	MGM
	Sworn Enemy	MGM
	The Longest Night	MGM
	Sinner Take All	MGM
	After the Thin Man (with Stothart)	MGM

1937	*Man of the People*	MGM
	Mama Steps Out	MGM
	The Good Old Soak	MGM
	Night Must Fall (O: Allen, Marquardt)	MGM
	Saratoga	MGM
	Bad Guy	MGM
	The Women Men Marry	MGM
	Double Wedding	MGM
	Live, Love and Learn	MGM
	The Last Gangster	MGM
	Navy Blue and Gold (O: Allen, Arnaud, Cutter; Navy Band arrangements: Marquardt)	MGM
1938	*Love Is a Headache*	MGM
	Mannequin	MGM
	Paradise for Three	MGM
	A Yank at Oxford (with Hubert Bath)	MGM
	Hold That Kiss	MGM
	The Toy Wife	MGM
	Lord Jeff	MGM
	The Shopworn Angel	MGM
	The Crown Roars	MGM
	The City of Little Men (short)	MGM
	Boys Town (O: Arnaud, Marquardt, Raab)	MGM
	Meet the Mayor	Times Exchange
	Vacation from Love	MGM
	Stablemates	MGM
1939	*Society Lawyer* (O: Arnaud)	MGM
	It's a Wonderful World	MGM
	6,000 Enemies	MGM
	Maisie	MGM
	Stronger Than Desire (with Snell)	MGM
	They All Come Out (with Snell)	MGM
	Andy Hardy Gets Spring Fever (with Snell)	MGM
	These Glamour Girls (with Snell; O: Heglin)	MGM
	The Women (with Snell; O: Heglin, Raab)	MGM
	Blackmail (with Snell)	MGM
	Thunder Afloat (with Snell)	MGM
	Dancing Co-ed (with Snell)	MGM
	Bad Little Angel	MGM
	Remember?	MGM
	Another Thin Man	MGM
	Joe and Ethel Turp Call on the President (with Snell)	MGM
	Nick Carter, Master Detective	MGM
1940	*Congo Maisie*	MGM
	Young Tom Edison	MGM

	My Son, My Son (O: Heglin, Raab, Schutt)	Small-UA
	South of Pago Pago	Small-UA
	Dance, Girl, Dance	RKO
	Kit Carson	Small-UA
1941	*The Son of Monte Cristo*	Small-UA
	Mr. and Mrs. Smith	RKO
	Cheers for Miss Bishop	Rowland-UA
	Tanks a Million	Roach-UA
	Niagara Falls	Roach-UA
	All-American Co-ed	Roach-UA
	Miss Polly	Roach-UA
1942	*Hay Foot*	Roach-UA
	Brooklyn Orchid	Roach-UA
	Dudes Are Pretty People	Roach-UA
	About Face	Roach-UA
	Flying with Music	Roach-UA
	Men of Texas	Universal
	The Devil with Hitler	Roach-UA
	The McGuerins from Brooklyn	Roach-UA
1943	*Calaboose*	Roach-UA
	Fall In	Roach-UA
	Taxi, Mister	Roach-UA
	Prairie Chickens	Roach-UA
	Yanks Ahoy	Roach-UA
	That Nazty Nuisance	Roach-UA
	Phantom of the Opera (O: Schutt, Zweifel)	Universal
	Moonlight in Vermont (MD)	Universal
1944	*Ali Baba and the Forty Thieves* (O: Zweifel)	Universal
	Her Primitive Man (MD)	Universal
	Cobra Woman (O: Zweifel)	Universal
	Ghost Catchers (MD; O: Zweifel)	Universal
	Gypsy Wildcat (O: Zweifel)	Universal
	The Climax (O: Zweifel)	Universal
	Bowery to Broadway	Universal
1945	*Frisco Sal* (MD; O: Zweifel)	Universal
	Song of the Sarong	Universal
	Salome, Where She Danced (O: Zweifel)	Universal
1947	*It Happened on Fifth Avenue*	Del Ruth-AA
	Copacabana	Coslow-UA
	(A: Bob Gordon, Jack Mason, Zweifel)	
1948	*The Babe Ruth Story*	Del Ruth-AA

FRANZ WAXMAN

1934	*Music in the Air* (MA)	Fox
1935	*Bride of Frankenstein*	Universal

	Diamond Jim	Universal
	The Affair of Susan	Universal
	His Night Out	Universal
	Three Kids and a Queen	Universal
	Remember Last Night?	Universal
	East of Java	Universal
	The Great Impersonation	Universal
1936	*Magnificent Obsession*	Universal
	The Invisible Ray	Universal
	Next Time We Love	Universal
	Love Before Breakfast	Universal
	Sutter's Gold	Universal
	Absolute Quiet	MGM
	Trouble for Two	MGM
	Fury	MGM
	The Devil Doll	MGM
	His Brother's Wife	MGM
	Love on the Run	MGM
1937	*Personal Property*	MGM
	A Day at the Races	MGM

(MD; A: Edens; O: Arnaud, Bassman, Marquardt)

	Captains Courageous	MGM
	The Emperor's Candlesticks	MGM
	The Bride Wore Red	MGM
1938	*Man-Proof*	MGM
	Arsene Lupin Returns	MGM
	Test Pilot	MGM
	Three Comrades	MGM
	Port of Seven Seas	MGM
	Too Hot to Handle	MGM
	The Young in Heart	Selznick-UA
	The Shining Hour	MGM
	Dramatic School	MGM
	A Christmas Carol	MGM
1939	*Honolulu*	MGM
	The Adventures of Huckleberry Finn	MGM
	The Ice Follies of 1939	MGM

(MD with Stoll; score: Edens; O: Arnaud, Bassman)

	Lucky Night	MGM
	On Borrowed Time	MGM
	Lady of the Tropics	MGM
	At the Circus (MD)	MGM
1940	*Strange Cargo*	MGM
	Florian	MGM
	Rebecca	Selznick-UA
	Sporting Blood	MGM

	I Love You Again	MGM
	Boom Town	MGM
	Escape	MGM
1941	*Flight Command*	MGM
	The Philadelphia Story	MGM
	Dr. Jekyll and Mr. Hyde	MGM
	Unfinished Business	Universal
	The Feminine Touch	MGM
	Honky Tonk	MGM
	Suspicion	RKO
	Design for Scandal	MGM
	Kathleen	MGM
1942	*The Woman of the Year*	MGM
	Tortilla Flat	MGM
	Her Cardboard Lover	MGM
	Seven Sweethearts	MGM
	Journey for Margaret (AC: Kaplan)	MGM
	Reunion in France	MGM
1943	*Air Force*	WB
	Edge of Darkness (O: Raab)	WB
	Old Acquaintance (O: Raab)	WB
1944	*Destination Tokyo* (O: Raab)	WB
	In Our Time	WB
	Mr. Skeffington (O: Raab)	WB
	The Very Thought of You (O: Arnaud)	WB
1945	*Objective, Burma* (O: Raab)	WB
	Hotel Berlin (O: Raab)	WB
	God Is My Co-Pilot (O: Moross)	WB
	The Horn Blows at Midnight (O: Raab)	WB
	Pride of the Marines (O: Raab)	WB
	Confidential Agent (O: Raab)	WB
1946	*Her Kind of Man* (O: Raab)	WB
1947	*Humoresque*	WB
	Nora Prentiss (O: Raab)	WB
	The Two Mrs. Carrolls (O: Raab)	WB
	Possessed (O: Raab)	WB
	Cry Wolf (O: Raab)	WB
	Dark Passage (O: Raab)	WB
	The Unsuspected (O: Raab)	WB
	That Hagen Girl (O: Raab)	WB
1948	*The Paradine Case*	Selznick-SRO
	Sorry, Wrong Number (O: Cutner, Shuken)	Paramount
	No Minor Vices	Enterprise-MGM
1949	*Whiplash* (O: Raab)	WB
	Alias Nick Beal	Paramount
	Night Unto Night (O: Raab)	WB

	Rope of Sand	Paramount
	Task Force (O: Raab)	WB
1950	*Johnny Holiday*	Alcorn-UA
	Night and the City (O: Powell)	20th
	The Furies (O: Cutner, Parrish, Raab, Shuken)	Paramount
	Sunset Boulevard (O: Cutner, Shuken)	Paramount
	Dark City	Paramount
1951	*Only the Valiant*	Cagney-WB
	He Ran All the Way	Roberts-UA
	A Place in the Sun (O: Cutner, Shuken)	Paramount
	The Blue Veil	Wald-Krasna-RKO
	Anne of the Indies (O: Powell)	20th
1952	*Decision Before Dawn* (O: Raab)	20th
	Phone Call from a Stranger (O: Mayers, Raab)	20th
	Red Mountain	Paramount
	Lure of the Wilderness (O: Raab)	20th
1953	*My Cousin Rachel* (O: Powell)	20th
	Come Back, Little Sheba	Paramount

ROY WEBB

1934	*Cockeyed Cavaliers*	RKO
	Kentucky Kernels	RKO
	Lightning Strikes Twice	RKO
1935	*Enchanted April*	RKO
	Captain Hurricane	RKO
	Laddie	RKO
	Strangers All	RKO
	The Nitwits	RKO
	The Arizonian	RKO
	Becky Sharp	RKO
	Old Man Rhythm	RKO
	The Last Days of Pompeii	RKO
	The Rainmakers	RKO
	Another Face	RKO
	We're Only Human	RKO
1936	*Sylvia Scarlett*	RKO
	The Lady Consents	RKO
	Muss 'Em Up	RKO
	Silly Billies	RKO
	Murder on a Bridle Path	RKO
	The Witness Chair	RKO
	Special Investigator	RKO
	The Ex-Mrs. Bradford	RKO

	Bunker Bean	RKO
	The Bride Walks Out	RKO
	Second Wife	RKO
	The Last of the Mohicans	Small-UA
	Mummy's Boys	RKO
	A Woman Rebels (O: De Packh)	RKO
1937	*The Plough and the Stars*	RKO
	Racing Lady	RKO
	Sea Devils	RKO
	Quality Street (O: De Packh)	RKO
	The Outcasts of Poker Flat	RKO
	Meet the Missus	RKO
	New Faces of 1937	RKO
	On Again—Off Again	RKO
	The Life of the Party	RKO
	Forty Naughty Girls	RKO
	Stage Door	RKO
	High Flyers	RKO
1938	*Bringing Up Baby*	RKO
	Night Spot	RKO
	Condemned Women	RKO
	Go Chase Yourself	RKO
	Vivacious Lady (O: Bennett)	RKO
	Gun Law	RKO
	Blond Cheat	RKO
	Border G-Man	RKO
	Having Wonderful Time	RKO
	Crime Ring	RKO
	Sky Giant	RKO
	I'm from the City	RKO
	Painted Desert	RKO
	The Affairs of Annabel	RKO
	The Renegade Ranger	RKO
	Room Service	RKO
	Mr. Doodle Kicks Off	RKO
	A Man to Remember	RKO
	The Mad Miss Manton	RKO
	Lawless Valley	RKO
	The Law West of Tombstone	RKO
	Next Time I Marry	RKO
1939	*The Great Man Votes*	RKO
	Arizona Legion	RKO
	Twelve Crowded Hours	RKO
	The Saint Strikes Back	RKO
	The Flying Irishman	RKO
	Trouble in Sundown	RKO

	Love Affair (O: Parrish)	RKO
	They Made Her a Spy	RKO
	Fixer Dugan	RKO
	The Rookie Cop	RKO
	Sorority House	RKO
	Panama Lady	RKO
	Racketeers of the Range	RKO
	The Girl from Mexico	RKO
	The Girl and the Gambler	RKO
	Five Came Back	RKO
	Timber Stampede	RKO
	Bachelor Mother	RKO
	Bad Lands	RKO
	In Name Only	RKO
	The Fighting Gringo	RKO
	Full Confession	RKO
	Three Sons	RKO
	Sued for Libel	RKO
	Reno	RKO
	Two Thoroughbreds	RKO
1940	*Married and in Love*	RKO
	The Saint's Double Trouble	RKO
	The Marines Fly High	RKO
	(MD; native music: Louis Betancourt)	
	Abe Lincoln in Illinois	RKO
	Curtain Call	RKO
	My Favorite Wife	RKO
	You Can't Fool Your Wife	RKO
	A Bill of Divorcement	RKO
	The Saint Takes Over	RKO
	Anne of Windy Poplars	RKO
	Cross Country Romance	RKO
	Millionaires in Prison	RKO
	One Crowded Night	RKO
	Stranger on the Third Floor	RKO
	I'm Still Alive	RKO
	Laddie	RKO
	Mexican Spitfire Out West	RKO
	You'll Find Out (MD; A: Duning)	RKO
	Kitty Foyle	RKO
1941	*Little Men*	RKO
	Let's Make Music (MD)	RKO
	The Saint in Palm Springs	RKO
	A Girl, a Guy and a Gob	RKO
	The Devil and Miss Jones	RKO
	Hurry, Charlie, Hurry	RKO

	Tom, Dick and Harry	RKO
	Parachute Battalion	RKO
	Father Takes a Wife	RKO
	Look Who's Laughing	RKO
	Weekend for Three	RKO
	Playmates (MD; A: Duning)	RKO
1942	*Obliging Young Lady*	RKO
	Joan of Paris	RKO
	The Tuttles of Tahiti	RKO
	My Favorite Spy (A: Duning)	RKO
	Powder Town	RKO
	Mexican Spitfire Sees a Ghost	RKO
	The Big Street	RKO
	Mexican Spitfire's Elephant	RKO
	Here We Go Again	RKO
	Highways by Night	RKO
	The Navy Comes Through	RKO
	I Married a Witch (O: Shuken)	Cinema Guild-UA
	The Falcon's Brother	RKO
	Seven Days' Leave	RKO
	Army Surgeon	RKO
	Cat People	RKO
1943	*Seven Miles from Alcatraz*	RKO
	Journey Into Fear	RKO
	Hitler's Children (O: De Packh)	RKO
	Flight for Freedom	RKO
	Ladies' Day	RKO
	I Walked with a Zombie	RKO
	The Falcon Strikes Back	RKO
	Bombardier (O: De Packh)	RKO
	Mr. Lucky	RKO
	The Leopard Man	RKO
	Petticoat Larceny	RKO
	The Falcon in Danger	RKO
	Behind the Rising Sun (O: De Packh	RKO
	A Lady Takes a Chance (O: De Packh)	RKO
	The Fallen Sparrow (O: De Packh)	RKO
	The Seventh Victim (O: De Packh)	RKO
	Gangway for Tomorrow	RKO
	The Iron Major (O: De Packh)	RKO
	The Ghost Ship	RKO
1944	*Passport to Destiny*	RKO
	The Curse of the Cat People	RKO
	Action in Arabia	RKO
	The Falcon Out West	RKO
	Marine Raiders (O: De Packh)	RKO

	Bride by Mistake	RKO
	The Seventh Cross (O: De Packh)	MGM
	Rainbow Island	Paramount
	Tall in the Saddle	RKO
	The Master Race	RKO
1945	*Experiment Perilous*	RKO
	Murder, My Sweet	RKO
	The Enchanted Cottage	RKO
	Betrayal from the East	RKO
	Those Endearing Young Charms	RKO
	Zombies on Broadway	RKO
	The Body Snatcher (O: Grau)	RKO
	Back to Bataan	RKO
	Two O'Clock Courage	RKO
	Love, Honor and Goodbye	Republic
	Cornered	RKO
	Dick Tracy	RKO
	The Spiral Staircase	RKO
1946	*Badman's Territory* (O: Grau)	RKO
	Bedlam	RKO
	The Well Groomed Bride	Paramount
	Without Reservations	RKO
	Notorious (O: Grau)	RKO
1947	*Easy Come, Easy Go* (O: Cutner, Shuken)	Paramount
	The Locket	RKO
	Sinbad the Sailor (O: Grau)	RKO
	They Won't Believe Me	RKO
	Crossfire	RKO
	Riffraff	RKO
	Magic Town	RKO
	Out of the Past	RKO
1948	*Cass Timberlane*	MGM
	I Remember Mama	RKO
	Fighting Father Dunne	RKO
	Race Street	RKO
	Rachel and the Stranger	RKO
	Blood on the Moon	RKO
1949	*Bad Men of Tombstone*	King Bros.-AA
	The Window	RKO
	Roughshod	RKO
	Mighty Joe Young	RKO
	Easy Living	RKO
	My Friend Irma (O: Cutner, Shuken)	Paramount
	Holiday Affair	RKO
1950	*The Secret Fury*	RKO
	The White Tower (O: Grau, Raab)	RKO

	Where Danger Lives (O: Grau, Raab)	RKO
	Vendetta	RKO
1951	*Branded* (O: Cutner, Shuken)	Paramount
	Gambling House	RKO
	Sealed Cargo	RKO
	Hard, Fast and Beautiful	RKO
	Flying Leathernecks	RKO
	Fixed Bayonets! (O: De Packh)	20th
1952	*A Girl in Every Port*	RKO
	At Sword's Point	RKO
	Clash by Night	RKO
	The Lusty Men	RKO
	Operation Secret (O: Cutner, Shuken)	WB

SHORTS—MUSICAL DIRECTION:

1934	*La Cucaracha*	RKO
	Bandits and Ballads	RKO
	Southern Style	RKO
	If This Isn't Love	RKO
1935	*Metropolitan Nocturne*	RKO
	(based on music by Louis Alter; O: Jackson)	
	The Spirit of 1976	RKO
	Ticket or Leave It	RKO
	Drawing Rumors	RKO
	A Night at the Biltmore Bowl	RKO
1936	*Lalapaloosa*	RKO
1937	*Singing in the Air*	RKO
	Swing Fever	RKO

KURT WEILL

1938	*You and Me* (AC: Harling; A: Boutelje, Roder)	Paramount

MEREDITH WILLSON

1940	*The Great Dictator*	Chaplin-UA
1941	*The Little Foxes*	Goldwyn-RKO

MORTIMER WILSON

1924	*The Thief of Bagdad*	Fairbanks-UA
1925	*Don Q*	Fairbanks-UA
1926	*The Black Pirate*	Fairbanks-UA

1948	*Sundown in Santa Fe*	Republic
	Renegades of Sonora	Republic
1949	*Rose of the Yukon*	Republic
	Sheriff of Wichita	Republic
	Daughter of the Jungle	Republic
	Hideout	Republic
	Duke of Chicago	Republic
	Death Valley Gunfighter	Republic
	Prince of the Plains	Republic
	Streets of San Francisco	Republic
	Frontier Investigator	Republic
	Law of the Golden West	Republic
	Outcasts of the Trail	Republic
	The Wyoming Bandit	Republic
	South of Rio	Republic
	Flaming Fury	Republic
	Bandit King of Texas	Republic
	Post Office Investigator	Republic
	Flame of Youth	Republic
	San Antone Ambush	Republic
	Navajo Trail Raiders	Republic
	Alias the Champ	Republic
	Ranger of Cherokee Strip	Republic
	Powder River Rustlers	Republic
	The Blonde Bandit	Republic
	Pioneer Marshal	Republic
1950	*Unmasked*	Republic
	Gunmen of Abilene	Republic
	Tarnished	Republic
	Belle of Old Mexico	Republic
	Federal Agent at Large	Republic
	Twilight in the Sierras (O: Butts)	Republic
	Code of the Silver Sage	Republic
	Harbor of Missing Men	Republic
	The Vanishing Westerner	Republic
	The Arizona Cowboy	Republic
	Hills of Oklahoma	Republic
	Salt Lake Raiders	Republic
	Destination Big House	Republic
	Covered Wagon Raid	Republic
	Trial Without Jury	Republic
	The Old Frontier	Republic
	Vigilante Hideout	Republic
	The Showdown	Republic
	Lonely Heart Bandits	Republic
	Frisco Tornado	Republic

Redwood Forest Trail	Republic
Prisoners in Petticoats	Republic
Rustlers on Horseback	Republic
Under Mexicali Stars	Republic
The Missourians	Republic

1951	*Pride of Maryland*	Republic
	Rough Riders of Durango	Republic
	Missing Women	Republic
	Night Riders of Montana	Republic
	Silver City Bonanza	Republic
	Cuban Fireball	Republic
	Insurance Investigator	Republic
	Thunder in God's Country	Republic
	Buckaroo Sheriff of Texas	Republic
	Wells Fargo Gunmaster	Republic
	Million Dollar Pursuit	Republic
	Secrets of Monte Carlo	Republic
	The Dakota Kid	Republic
	Rodeo King and the Senorita	Republic
	Fort Dodge Stampede	Republic
	Havana Rose	Republic
	Arizona Manhunt	Republic
	Utah Wagon Train	Republic
	Street Bandits	Republic
	The Desert of Lost Men	Republic
	Pals of the Golden West	Republic

1952	*Woman in the Dark*	Republic
	Captive of Billy the Kid	Republic
	Leadville Gunslinger	Republic
	The Fabulous Senorita	Republic
	Gobs and Gals	Republic
	Old Oklahoma Plains	Republic
	Tropical Heat Wave	Republic
	Desperadoes' Outpost	Republic
	South Pacific Trail	Republic

SAM WINELAND

1933	*Samarang*	Zeidman-UA
1935	*Smart Girl* (MD)	Paramount
	Every Night at Eight (MD; O: Mertz)	Paramount
	Legong: Dance of the Virgins (MD)	Paramount
1937	*When's Your Birthday?*	Loew-RKO

CHARLES WOLCOTT

1944	*The Three Caballeros*	Disney-RKO
	(MD with Plumb, Smith)	
1946	*Make Mine Music*	Disney-RKO
	(MD; associates: Ken Darby, Plumb, Wallace)	

Also many Disney cartoons.

VICTOR YOUNG

ARRANGEMENTS:

1936	*Anything Goes*	Paramount
	Klondike Annie	Paramount
	Frankie and Johnnie	Republic
	Three Cheers for Love	Paramount
	The Big Broadcast of 1937	Paramount
	College Holiday	Paramount
1937	*Turn Off the Moon* (with Boutelje)	Paramount
	Mountain Music	Paramount
	Double or Nothing (with Terr)	Paramount
1938	*Thrill of a Lifetime* (with Franklin)	Paramount

SCORE:

1936	*Fatal Lady* (with Carbonara)	Paramount
1937	*Champagne Waltz*	Paramount
	(also arrangements with Boutelje)	
	Maid of Salem	Paramount
	Swing High, Swing Low	Paramount
	(also arrangements with Boutelje)	
	Vogues of 1938	Wanger-UA
	Ebb Tide	Paramount
	Wells Fargo	Paramount
1938	*Army Girl*	Republic
	The Gladiator	Loew-Col
	Breaking the Ice	Principal-RKO
	Peck's Bad Boy with the Circus	Principal-RKO
	Flirting with Fate	Loew-MGM
1939	*Fisherman's Wharf*	Principal-RKO
	Man of Conquest	Republic
	Heritage of the Desert	Paramount
	Man About Town (MD)	Paramount
	Way Down South	Principal-RKO
	Golden Boy (O: Shuken)	Columbia
	Our Neighbors, the Carters	Paramount
	The Night of Nights	Paramount
	The Llano Kid	Paramount
	Escape to Paradise (MD)	Principal-RKO

	Gulliver's Travels (O: Shuken)	Paramount
	Raffles	Goldwyn-UA
1940	*The Light That Failed* (O: Shuken)	Paramount
	Knights of the Range (with Leipold)	Paramount
	Road to Singapore	Paramount
	The Dark Command	Republic
	The Light of Western Stars	Paramount
	Buck Benny Rides Again (O: Shuken)	Paramount
	Those Were the Days	Paramount
	The Way of All Flesh	Paramount
	Three Faces West	Republic
	Untamed	Paramount
	Rhythm on the River (MD; A: Franklin)	Paramount
	I Want a Divorce	Paramount
	Moon Over Burma	Paramount
	Dancing on a Dime (MD)	Paramount
	Arise My Love	Paramount
	Three Men from Texas	Paramount
	Arizona (O: Cutner)	Columbia
	North West Mounted Police	Paramount
	Love Thy Neighbor (MD; A: Franklin)	Paramount
1941	*The Mad Doctor*	Paramount
	Las Vegas Nights (MD)	Paramount
	Road to Zanzibar	Paramount
	Reaching for the Sun	Paramount
	I Wanted Wings	Paramount
	Caught in the Draft	Paramount
	Kiss the Boys Goodbye (MD)	Paramount
	Aloma of the South Seas	Paramount
	Hold Back the Dawn	Paramount
	Skylark	Paramount
	Glamour Boy (MD)	Paramount
1942	*The Fleet's In* (MD; PS: Shuken)	Paramount
	The Remarkable Andrew	Paramount
	The Great Man's Lady	Paramount
	True to the Army (MD)	Paramount
	Reap the Wild Wind	Paramount
	Take a Letter, Darling	Paramount
	Sweater Girl (MD)	Paramount
	Beyond the Blue Horizon	Paramount
	Priorities on Parade (MD)	Paramount
	The Glass Key	Paramount
	Flying Tigers	Republic
	The Forest Rangers (AC: Carbonara)	Paramount
	Road to Morocco	Paramount
	Mrs. Wiggs of the Cabbage Patch	Paramount

	Silver Queen	Sherman-UA
1943	*The Palm Beach Story*	Paramount
	My Heart Belongs to Daddy (MD)	Paramount
	The Crystal Ball	Cinema Guild-UA
	Young and Willing	Cinema Guild-UA
	The Outlaw	Hughes-UA
	China	Paramount
	Salute for Three (MD)	Paramount
	Buckskin Frontier	Sherman-UA
	True to Life	Paramount
	Hostages	Paramount
	Riding High (MD)	Paramount
	For Whom the Bell Tolls (O: Parrish, Shuken)	Paramount
1944	*No Time for Love*	Paramount
	The Uninvited (O: Shuken)	Paramount
	And the Angels Sing (MD)	Paramount
	The Great Moment	Paramount
	The Story of Dr. Wassell	Paramount
	And Now Tomorrow	Paramount
	Frenchman's Creek (O: Parrish, Shuken)	Paramount
	Ministry of Fear	Paramount
1945	*Practically Yours*	Paramount
	Out of This World (MD)	Paramount
	The Great John L.	Crosby-UA
	A Medal for Benny	Paramount
	You Came Along*	Paramount
	Love Letters*	Paramount
	Hold That Blonde*	Paramount
1946	*Kitty*	Paramount
	Masquerade in Mexico (MD)*	Paramount
	The Blue Dahlia	Paramount
	Our Hearts Were Growing Up	Paramount
	To Each His Own*	Paramount
	The Searching Wind*	Paramount
	Two Years Before the Mast	Paramount
1947	*California**	Paramount
	Suddenly It's Spring*	Paramount
	The Imperfect Lady*	Paramount
	Calcutta*	Paramount
	The Trouble with Women (with Dolan)*	Paramount
	Golden Earrings*	Paramount
	Unconquered*	Paramount
1948	*I Walk Alone**	Paramount
	The Big Clock*	Paramount

---

* Orchestrations: Sidney Cutner, Leo Shuken.

	*State of the Union**	Liberty-MGM
	The Emperor Waltz (O: Hallenbeck)*	Paramount
	*Dream Girl**	Paramount
	So Evil My Love (with Wm. Alwyn)*	Paramount
	*Beyond Glory**	Paramount
	*Night Has a Thousand Eyes**	Paramount
	*Miss Tatlock's Millions**	Paramount
	*The Paleface**	Paramount
1949	*The Accused**	Paramount
	A Connecticut Yankee in King Arthur's Court (O: Van Cleave)*	Paramount
	*Streets of Laredo**	Paramount
	Song of Surrender	Paramount
	*Samson and Delilah**	Paramount
	Chicago Deadline	Paramount
1950	*Thelma Jordan**	Paramount
	*My Foolish Heart**	Goldwyn-RKO
	*Deadly Is the Female**	King Bros.-UA
	*Sands of Iwo Jima**	Republic
	*Paid in Full**	Paramount
	Riding High (MD)	Paramount
	*Bright Leaf**	WB
	*Our Very Own**	Goldwyn-RKO
	*The Fireball**	Thor-20th
	Rio Grande	Argosy-Rep
1951	*Belle Le Grand*	Republic
	Payment on Demand	Skirball-Manning-RKO
	September Affair (O: Parrish)*	Paramount
	*The Lemon Drop Kid**	Paramount
	*Appointment with Danger**	Paramount
	Bullfighter and the Lady	Republic
	This Is Korea (doc.)	Republic
	*A Millionaire for Christy**	Thor-20th
	Honeychile	Republic
	*My Favorite Spy**	Paramount
	The Wild Blue Yonder	Republic
1952	*Something to Live For**	Paramount
	*Anything Can Happen**	Paramount
	Scaramouche	MGM
	*The Greatest Show on Earth**	Paramount
	*The Story of Will Rogers**	WB
	One Minute to Zero	RKO
	*The Quiet Man**	Argosy-Rep
	Thunderbirds	Republic

---

* Orchestrations: Sidney Cutner, Leo Shuken.

	Blackbeard the Pirate	RKO
1953	*The Star*	Friedlob-20th
	The Stars Are Singing	Paramount
	Shane	Paramount

LEE ZAHLER

1930	*Pure and Simple* (short)	Darmour-Radio
1931	*A Private Scandal*	Headline
1932	*The Silver Lining*	Patrician-UA
	Big Business (short)	RKO
	Mickey's Golden Rule (short)	RKO
	The Vanishing Frontier	Darmour-Par
1933	*Campus Codes* (short)	Columbia
	Laughing at Life	Mascot
	Marriage Humor (short)	Paramount
1935	*Symphony of Living*	Invincible
	Public Opinion	Invincible
	The Fire Trap	Empire
	Motive for Revenge	Majestic
	The Unknown Ranger	Columbia
	Just My Luck	New Century-Corona
	The Lost City	Regal
1936	*Shadows of the Orient*	Empire
	North of Nome	Columbia
	Slander House	Progressive
1937	*The Lash of the Penitentes*	Telepictures
	Little Jack Horner (short)	Columbia
	The Boy Who Saved a Nation (short)	Columbia
	Silver Threads (short)	Columbia
	The Herald of the Skies (short)	Columbia
	The Fifty Year Barter (short)	Columbia
1938	*Stagecoach Days*	Columbia
	Pioneer Trail	Columbia
1939	*The Law Comes to Texas*	Columbia
	Hidden Power	Columbia
1940	*Outside the 3-Mile Limit*	Columbia
	Passport to Alcatraz	Columbia
	Ellery Queen, Master Detective	Columbia
	The Great Plane Robbery	Columbia
1941	*Ellery Queen's Penthouse Mystery*	Columbia
	The Great Swindle	Columbia
	Ellery Queen and the Perfect Crime	Columbia
	Ellery Queen and the Murder Ring	Columbia
1942	*A Close Call for Ellery Queen*	Columbia

	A Desperate Chance for Ellery Queen	Columbia
	Gallant Lady	PRC
	Bombs Over Burma	PRC
	Enemy Agents Meet Ellery Queen	Columbia
	The Yanks Are Coming	PRC
	Miss V from Moscow	PRC
	Captain Midnight (serial)	Columbia
	Perils of the Royal Mounted (serial)	Columbia
1943	*Man of Courage*	PRC
	No Place for a Lady	Columbia
	The Ghost and the Guest	PRC
	A Gentle Gangster	Republic
	Crime Doctor	Columbia
	Tiger Fangs	PRC
	The Underdog	PRC
	The Crime Doctor's Strangest Case	Columbia
	The Batman (serial)	Columbia
	The Phantom (serial)	Columbia
1944	*Gunsmoke Mesa*	PRC
	Men on Her Mind	PRC
	Shake Hands with Murder	PRC
	The Pinto Bandit	PRC
	Waterfront	PRC
	Brand of the Devil	PRC
	Seven Doors to Death	PRC
	Delinquent Daughters	PRC
	Gangsters of the Frontier	PRC
	Shadow of Suspicion	Supreme-Mon
	I Accuse My Parents	PRC
	The Great Mike	PRC
	Masked for Murder	PRC
	Rogues Gallery	PRC
	Black Arrow (serial)	Columbia
1945	*Boss of Rawhide*	PRC
	Hollywood and Vine	PRC
	Enemy of the Law	PRC
	The Lady Confesses	PRC
	Three in the Saddle	PRC
	Jeep-Herders	Planet
	Frontier Fugitives	PRC
	Arson Squad	PRC
	Prairie Rustlers	PRC
	Navajo Kid	PRC
	The Monster and the Ape (serial)	Columbia
	Jungle Raiders (serial)	Columbia
	Who's Guilty?	Columbia

1946	*Detour to Danger*	Planet
	Six Gun for Hire	PRC
	Lightning Raiders	PRC
	Ambush Trail	PRC
	Gentlemen with Guns	PRC
	Thunder Town	PRC
	Prairie Badmen	PRC
	Overland Riders	PRC
	Hop Harrigan (serial)	Columbia
	Son of the Guardsman (serial)	Columbia
1947	*Jack Armstrong* (serial)	Columbia
	Queen of the Amazons	Screen Art-SG

EDWARD KILENYI

1937	*Zamboanga*	Filippine-GN
	Headin' East	Columbia
1938	*Adventures of Chico*	Woodard-Mon
	Topa Topa	Pennant
	The Overland Express	Coronet-Col
	International Crime	Grand National
	Two Gun Justice	Monogram
	The Terror of Tiny Town	Principal-Col
1942	*Ravaged Earth*	
1947	*The Tender Years*	Alson-20th
1948	*Belle Starr's Daughter*	Alson-20th

OSCAR LEVANT

1934	*Crime Without Passion* (with Tours)	Paramount
1937	*Charlie Chan at the Opera* (opera sequence)	20th
	Nothing Sacred	Selznick-UA
1939	*Made for Each Other* (PS)	Selznick-UA

DARIUS MILHAUD

1947	*The Private Affairs of Bel Ami*	Loew-Lewin-UA
1948	*Dreams That Money Can Buy*	Films Intl. of America
	(with Applebaum, Bowles, Cage, Diamond)	

WILLIAM FREDERICK PETERS

1920	*Way Down East* (with Silvers)	Griffith-UA
1922	*Orphans of the Storm*	UA
	When Knighthood Was in Flower	Paramount

1923	*Enemies of Women*	Goldwyn
	Little Old New York	Goldwyn
	Under the Red Robe	Goldwyn
1924	*Yolande*	MGM
1929	*The Four Feathers*	Paramount
	The Hungarian Rhapsody	Paramount

ERNO RAPEE

1927	*Sunrise* (O: Baron)	Fox
1928	*Street Angel* (O: Baron)	Fox
	Four Sons (O: Baron)	Fox
	Fazil	Fox
	Red Dance	Fox
1929	*Whispering Winds*	T-S
	The River (O: Baron)	Fox
1930	*Old English*	WB
	Going Wild	WB
1931	*A Connecticut Yankee*	Fox
	Over the Hill	Fox
1934	*Chloe*	Pinnacle
1937	*The Dead March*	Imperial
1939	*Back Door to Heaven*	Paramount

FRANK TOURS

1933	*The Emperor Jones*	UA
1934	*Crime Without Passion* (with Levant)	Paramount
	Gambling	Fox
1937	*Fight for Your Lady*	RKO
	She's Got Everything	RKO
1938	*Everybody's Doing It*	RKO
	Mother Carey's Chickens	RKO
	Smashing the Rackets	RKO
	Tarnished Angel	RKO
	The Duke of West Point	Small-UA
1939	*Boy Slaves*	RKO
	King of the Turf	Small-UA
	Beauty for the Asking	RKO
	Almost a Gentleman	RKO
	Conspiracy	RKO
1940	*Beyond Tomorrow*	RKO
	Men Against the Sky	RKO
	The Villain Still Pursued Her	RKO

1934 Louis Silvers, *One Night of Love* (Columbia)

1935 Max Steiner, *The Informer* (RKO)

1936 Erich Wolfgang Korngold, *Anthony Adverse* (Warner Bros.)

1937 Charles Previn, *One Hundred Men and a Girl* (Universal)

1938 (Original Score) Erich Wolfgang Korngold, *The Adventures of Robin Hood* (Warner Bros.)

(Score) Alfred Newman, *Alexander's Ragtime Band* (20th Century-Fox)

1939 (Original Score) Herbert Stothart, *The Wizard of Oz* (MGM)

(Score) Richard Hageman, W. Franke Harling, John Leipold, Leo Shuken, *Stagecoach* (UA)

1940 (Original Score) Leigh Harline, Paul Smith, *Pinocchio* (Disney)

(Score) Alfred Newman, *Tin Pan Alley* (20th Century-Fox)

1941 (Drama) Bernard Herrmann, *All That Money Can Buy* (RKO)

(Musical) Frank Churchill, Oliver Wallace, *Dumbo* (Disney)

1942 (Drama) Max Steiner, *Now, Voyager* (Warner Bros.)

(Musical) Ray Heindorf, Heinz Roemheld, *Yankee Doodle Dandy* (Warner Bros.)

1943 (Drama) Alfred Newman, *The Song of Bernadette* (20th Century-Fox)

(Musical) Ray Heindorf, *This Is the Army* (Warner Bros.)

1944 (Drama) Max Steiner, *Since You Went Away* (Selznick)

(Musical) Carmen Dragon, *Cover Girl* (Columbia)

1945 (Drama) Miklos Rozsa, *Spellbound* (Selznick)

(Musical) Georgie Stoll, *Anchors Aweigh* (MGM)

1946 (Drama) Hugo Friedhofer, *The Best Years of Our Lives* (Goldwyn)

(Musical) Morris Stoloff, *The Jolson Story* (Columbia)

1947 (Drama) Miklos Rozsa, *A Double Life* (Universal)

(Musical) Alfred Newman, *Mother Wore Tights* (20th Century-Fox)

1948 (Drama) Brian Easdale, *The Red Shoes* (Archers)

(Musical) Johnny Green, Roger Edens, *Easter Parade* (MGM)

1949 (Drama) Aaron Copland, *The Heiress* (Paramount)
(Musical) Lennie Hayton, Roger Edens, *On the Town* (MGM)

1950 (Drama) Franz Waxman, *Sunset Boulevard* (Paramount)
(Musical) Adolph Deutsch, Roger Edens, *Annie Get Your Gun* (MGM)

1951 (Drama) Franz Waxman, *A Place in the Sun* (Paramount)
(Musical) Johnny Green, Saul Chaplin, *An American in Paris* (MGM)

1952 (Drama) Dimitri Tiomkin, *High Noon* (UA)
(Musical) Alfred Newman, *With a Song in My Heart* (20th Century-Fox)

1953 (Drama) Bronislau Kaper, *Lili* (MGM)
(Musical) Alfred Newman, *Call Me Madam* (20th Century-Fox)

1954 (Drama) Dimitri Tiomkin, *The High and the Mighty* (Warner Bros.)
(Musical) Adolph Deutsch, Saul Chaplin, *Seven Brides for Seven Brothers* (MGM)

1955 (Drama) Alfred Newman, *Love Is a Many-Splendored Thing* (20th Century-Fox)
(Musical) Robert Russell Bennett, Jay Blackton, Adolph Deutsch, *Oklahoma!* (Magna)

1956 (Drama) Victor Young, *Around the World in 80 Days* (UA)
(Musical) Alfred Newman, Ken Darby, *The King and I* (20th Century-Fox)

1957 Malcolm Arnold, *The Bridge on the River Kwai* (Columbia)

1958 (Drama) Dimitri Tiomkin, *The Old Man and the Sea* (Warner Bros.)
(Musical) Andre Previn, *Gigi* (MGM)

1959 (Drama) Miklos Rozsa, *Ben-Hur* (MGM)
(Musical) Andre Previn, Ken Darby, *Porgy and Bess* (Goldwyn)

1960 (Drama) Ernest Gold, *Exodus* (UA)
(Musical) Harry Sukman, *Song Without End* (Columbia)

1961 (Drama) Henry Mancini, *Breakfast at Tiffany's* (Paramount)
(Musical) Saul Chaplin, Johnny Green, Irwin Kostal, Sid Ramin, *West Side Story* (UA)

1962 (Original) Maurice Jarre, *Lawrence of Arabia* (Columbia)
(Adaptation) Ray Heindorf, *The Music Man* (Warner Bros.)

1963   (Original) John Addison, *Tom Jones* (Woodfall)

      (Adaptation) Andre Previn, *Irma La Douce* (UA)

1964   (Original) Richard M. Sherman, Robert B. Sherman, *Mary Poppins* (Disney)

      (Adaptation) Andre Previn, *My Fair Lady* (Warner Bros.)

1965   (Original) Maurice Jarre, *Doctor Zhivago* (MGM)

      (Adaptation) Irwin Kostal, *The Sound of Music* (20th Century-Fox)

1966   (Original) John Barry, *Born Free* (Columbia)

      (Adaptation) Ken Thorne, *A Funny Thing Happened on the Way to the Forum* (UA)

1967   (Original) Elmer Bernstein, *Thoroughly Modern Millie* (Universal)

      (Adaptation) Alfred Newman, Ken Darby, *Camelot* (Warner Bros.)

1968   (Drama) John Barry, *The Lion in Winter* (Avco Embassy)

      (Musical) Johnny Green, *Oliver!* (Columbia)

1969   (Drama) Burt Bacharach, *Butch Cassidy and the Sundance Kid* (20th Century-Fox)

      (Musical) Lennie Hayton, Lionel Newman, *Hello, Dolly!* (20th Century-Fox)

1970   (Score) Francis Lai, *Love Story* (Paramount)

      (Song Score) The Beatles, *Let It Be* (UA)

1971   (Original) Michel Legrand, *Summer of '42* (Warner Bros.)

      (Adaptation) John Williams, *Fiddler on the Roof* (UA)

INDEX OF FILM TITLES

145

147

148

149

151

152

153

156

157

Girl of the Ozarks, 13
Girl on the Bridge, The, 11
Girl Trouble, 72
Girl Without a Room, 49
Girls' Dormitory, 58
Girls in Chains, 26
Girls of Pleasure Island, The, 69
Girls of the Big House, 23
Girl's School, 114
Give Us This Night, 55
Give Us Wings, 85
Gladiator, The, 134
Glamour, 49
Glamour Boy, 135
Glamour in Tennis, 51
Glass Alibi, The, 59
Glass Key, The, 135
Glass Menagerie, The, 111
Glimpses of Australia, 96
Glory Alley, 114
Go Chase Yourself, 127
Go for Broke!, 17
Go Into Your Dance, 45
Go West, 113
Gobs and Gals, 133
God Is My Co-Pilot, 125
God's Country and the Woman, 109
Goin' to Town, 95
Going Hollywood, 115
Going My Way, 22
Going Places, 45
Gold Diggers in Paris, 45
Gold Diggers of 1937, 45
Gold Is Where You Find It, 109
Gold Mine in the Sky, 17
Gold Rush, The, 15
Gold Rush Maisie, 103
Golden Arrow, The, 43
Golden Boy, 134
Golden Earrings, 136
Golden Fleecing, The, 103
Golden Gloves, 56
Golden Gloves Story, The, 59
Golden Harvest, 80
Golden Hoofs, 67
Golden Horde, The, 88
Golden Stallion, The, 94
Goldwyn Follies, The, 32
Gone with the Wind, 109
Good Earth, The, 116
Good Fellows, The, 97
Good Humor Man, The, 81
Good Luck, Mr. Yates, 63
Good News, 44
Good Old Corn, 61
Good Old Soak, The, 122
Good Sam, 22
Goodbye, My Fancy, 2
Gorgeous Hussy, The, 116
Gorilla, The, 8

Government Girl, 40
Gracie Allen Murder Case, The, 13
Grand Canary, 19
Grand Canyon, 33
Grand Canyon Trail, 94
Grand Central Murder, 104
Grand Jury, 16
Grand Old Girl, 16
Grand Ole Opry, 28
Grandad of Races, 62
Grandpa Goes to Town, 28
Grapes of Wrath, The, 71
Grass Is Always Greener, The, 62
Great American Broadcast, The, 72
Great Caruso, The, 37
Great Dan Patch, The, 93
Great Dictator, The, 15
Great Expectations, 121
Great Flamarion, The, 59
Great Gabbo, The, 49
Great Garrick, The, 19
Great Gatsby, The, 22
Great Gildersleeve, The, 89
Great Guy, 98
Great Heart, The, 105
Great Impersonation, The (1935), 124
Great Impersonation, The (1942), 86
Great Jaspar, The, 107
Great Jewel Robber, The, 60
Great John L., The, 136
Great Lie, The, 110
Great Lover, The, 64
Great Man Votes, The, 127
Great Man's Lady, The, 135
Great McGinty, The, 48
Great Mike, The, 139
Great Missouri Raid, The, 91
Great Mr. Nobody, The, 20
Great Moment, The, 136
Great Plane Robbery, The, 138
Great Profile, The, 66
Great Rupert, The, 112
Great Sinner, The, 52
Great Swindle, The, 138
Great Train Robbery, The, 29
Great Victor Herbert, The, 58
Great Waltz, The, 118
Great Wilderness, The, 99
Great Ziegfeld, The, 58
Greatest Show on Earth, The, 137
Greeks Had a Word for Them, The, 70
Green Cockatoo, The, 82
Green Dolphin Street, 52
Green Grass of Wyoming, 67
Green Light, 109
Green Pastures, The, 55
Green Promise, The, 93

159

162

170

172

175

178

181

182

184

187

189

INDEX OF ORCHESTRATORS

(Also included are arrangers, adaptors, and some additional composers.)

191

192

INDEX OF ORCHESTRATORS

(Also included are arrangers, adaptors, and some additional composers.)

191

192